# DISCOVERING DUNSTER

by

## HILARY BINDING

For Ned

THE EXMOOR PRESS

'I am at last returned from my Somersetshire expedition... I think the country abounds with beautiful prospects... I was mightily pleased with Dunster Castle, near Minehead. It stands upon a great eminence, and hath a prospect of that town, with an extensive view of the Bristol Channel, in which are seen two small islands, the Steep Holmes and the Flat Holmes, and on t'other side we plainly distinguished the divisions of fields on the Welsh coast. All the journey I performed on horseback'
John Gray. 1732

'We passed Dunster on our right, a small town between the brow of a hill and the sea. I remember eyeing it wistfully as it lay below us, contrasted with the woody scene around, it looked as clear, as pure, as embrowned and ideal as any landscape I have seen since .....'
William Hazlitt. My First Acquaintance with Poets. 1823

'Dunster town standith in a botom. The paroch church is set in ground somewhat rising. There is a very celebrate market at Dunstorre ons a wekes. There is a fair privilegid to be at Dunster every Whitsun Mone-day. The town of Dunnestorre makith cloth. The Moions buildid the right goodly and strong castelle of Dunnestorre'
John Leland. 1538

'A little Markett Towne seated on a flatt altogether environed with hills except towards ye Sea... Sir John Lutterell, whose faire house built on ye Castell Mount is the greatest ornament of ye Place.'

# CHAPTER 1

# Dunster Town Looking Back

Fifteen hundred years before Dunster Castle was built people were living on the hills above the River Avill in scattered, undefended homesteads, growing crops in small fields and keeping tough and wiry sheep, goats and pigs. Round about 350 B.C. these peaceful users of bronze and iron were forced to build the round enclosure on Gallox Hill where they could retreat, with their animals, and repel the attacks of invaders originating from North and West France. Bat's Castle nearby is a more complex fortification and may have been built as a response to later, more severe attacks.

Tradition links the Romans with Bat's Castle but apart from a few coins found in the vicinity there is no evidence for this. Once Britain was settled under Roman rule, Roman coinage was current and any passing Briton might have dropped the odd denarius.

*Bat's Castle with the earlier enclosure in the distance.*

No one has yet claimed Dunster as the site of Camelot but it does have its own King Arthur legend told in a Latin life of St. Carantoc, original patron of neighbouring Carhampton. St. Carantoc decided that he would choose an area for missionary work by throwing his portable altar stone into the Severn and following by boat to wherever it went ashore. However he lost track of the stone and during his search of the West Somerset coast, came across Cato and Arthur, princes in the area, who were living at Dindrarthou (identified with Dunster). Nearby in the region of Carrum (Carhampton) a ferocious serpent was ravaging the land, a threat to all. Arthur by now had found the altar stone and intended to use it as a table but unfortunately anything placed on it was immediately thrown off. Carantoc enquired after his altar which was restored to him in return for his capturing and taming the serpent.

Whatever the tale's credibility it may be an indication that there was a settlement of some note in the Dunster area during the period known as the Dark Ages.

The first Saxons invaded the area around 700 A.D. and soon settled the present Dunster site. The first written reference in Domesday book names the town Torre (tor) but it was probably called after a Saxon thane, Dunna, who founded the settlement with its central strategically placed hill. Tradition suggests that there was a Saxon fortress on the tor but there is no evidence of this. The last Saxon lord of Dunster was Aluric who also held the neighbouring manors of Avill and Broadwood and Bratton on the other side of Minehead.

One of William of Normandy's chief supporters in his conquest of England was William de Mohun who came from St.Lo, not far from Bayeux in Normandy. After the Battle of Hastings in 1066 William was granted sixty-nine West Country manors including Dunster where he decided to build the castle which was to become the administrative centre of his estates.

Dunster was only a small manor. The Domesday survey of 1086 records only enough ploughland for one plough, five acres of meadow and thirty acres of pasture. Fifteen bordars (cottagers) with their families worked the strips of arable land in fields to the west of the town.

However, two points indicate that the survey does not tell the whole story. The lord's tenants were expected to grind their corn at his mill. There are two mills mentioned in Dunster implying use by or for larger numbers than usual. Also, the value of the manor had risen by 200% from 5s in 1066 to 15s in 1086 almost certainly because of the work and trade brought to Dunster by the building of the castle, details not asked for in the survey. The population of Dunster must have been larger than the Domesday agricultural return implies.

*The Castle dominates the town.*

William's choice of Dunster as the site for his castle was the making of the town. In 1197 it was described as a borough and by 1222 known to have a market. In 1253, Reginald de Mohun, the lord of the manor, granted the burgesses of Dunster the right to hold markets and fairs "in North Street freely and quietly and fully" for ever. In return the burgesses gave him a tun (252 gallons) of wine worth 40s, perhaps pressed from grapes grown in the vineyards on the sunny south-facing slopes of Grabbist Hill.

The next year the burgesses were granted various privileges including some tax exemptions. Later charters granted the right to "have furze, whorts, turfs, fern and heath sufficient for their fuel" on Croydon Hill, slime from the marsh (for improving their land) and common rights of pasture for their plough-cattle except on

*Dunster Town from the air showing the medieval burgages.*

'Estmersh', 40 acres used as a rabbit warren and known as Coleborrowes. This area replaced the old warren or 'coney-garth' on Conygar Hill from which the rabbits could easily reach and ravage the town's gardens. Rabbit was a welcome addition to the medieval diet but seems to have been a problem at the time for burgesses were allowed to kill them freely so long as they took the skins to the Castle.

Burgesses were those people who held a burgage. These were narrow strips of land generally running at right angles to the street with enough ground for house and garden. The burgages in the High Street were separated on the east from the Hanger Park and on the west from Priory Green, by a continuous wall or wooden paling and many can still be identified. Burgesses paid a rent to the lord of a shilling a year and a 'boroughright' or toll when a burgage was transferred. They were, in effect, free men, able to do what they liked with their burgages. They could bequeath them and prosperous tradesmen might acquire more than one in order to extend their business. The surnames of burgesses in 1266 hint that the town was growing as a centre of craftsmanship and trade.

Mazun, Smith, Carpenter, Poter, Baker, Webber, Fuller, Tanner, Corour (leather dresser), Glover, Chapman (pedlar) Millar, Gardiner, Fisher, Hunter, Dyer.

During this period sea-going ships harboured in the mouth of the river Avill. The Northpulle (North Pill) was close to the Foghelrismersh (Fowler's Marsh) and the inhabitants of the northern part of the town, now Dunster Marsh, would have worked in maritime occupations including fishing and ship-building. In 1375 one of 39 ships captured by the French in the Bay of Bourgneuf was the St. Marie Cog of Dunster while in 1418 the 'Leonard of Dounsterre, barge of the noble lord the Lord Hugh Luttrell, Knight, Lord of Donnstre, whereof is master Philip Clapton' sailed to Bordeaux returning with a cargo of French wine.

Fishing was carried on both on- and off-shore. Foreshore fishing rights belonged to the lord of the manor and there were numerous fisheries, both weirs and pools, between Minehead and Blue Anchor. A weir was a low stone wall set with stakes and woven with wattles like a fence. It was generally built in the form of an angle with the apex towards the withdrawing tide line to contain the fish. They were built in two rows, one for neap, one for spring tides and demanded constant maintenance. The income from these weirs was considerable and the right to hold one jealously guarded.

In the 16th century Dunster Haven was still a creek frequented by 'small botes' and in 1566 the Mychael 'of Donstarre', master John Will, carried wool from Milford in Wales to Dunster. When Gerard of Trent visited Dunster in 1633 he noted the number of boats from Ireland visiting the 'pretty harbour' but no sign of the harbour remains for the whole river estuary has silted up. It is likely that boats were once able to navigate the tidal estuary of the Avill and tie up at the foot of the castle tor. The writer of Gesta Stephani speaks of the water lapping the foot of the tor. Archaeological investigation could confirm or deny the theory.

Our newspapers these days are full of bad news and things that people have done wrong. Similarly many of the documents dating from the medieval period record the proceedings of the courts. The lord's steward always

*Dunster Market and Shambles about 1800. This artist's impression was photographed about 1870. The white lines are cracks in the glass plate.*

presided and a jury of twelve freemen attended the two principal courts held each year soon after Easter and Michaelmas. Borough officers were elected annually including two constables of the peace, two bread-weighers and two ale-tasters and later keepers of the shambles and keepers of the streets. The constables reported all breaches of the peace, the bread-weighers presented those who sold bread of short weight and poor quality (perhaps adulterated with chalk) and the ale-tasters those whose beer was not up to scratch. . Butchers and fishermen were expected to sell their goods in the local market and might be fined if they didn't. Among the responsibilities of the street-keepers was keeping them free of straying animals which if impounded could only be released on payment of a fee.

By 1423 a range of open stalls had been built in the centre of North Street to augment the number of permanent shops and to provide for the ever-growing body of customers. Users of these stalls paid dues to the bailiffs while the keepers of the Shambles with the other officers helped regulate the business of the market.

Offenders were tried at the 'pie-powder'(dusty feet) court which from 1426 was held in the wooden building which served as Town Hall.

Some offences seem fairly petty but devolved from a real need to 'keep the peace' in an insular community as these examples show. In 1408 Ellen Watkyns was charged with being a 'common 'holcroppe' '(petty pilferer)' of divers things and a common scold and disturber of the peace'. In 1443 John Towker was presented as a 'common spy or listener at the windows of the neighbours and likewise a common night-walker and eavesdropper' and in 1493 the wives of John Huyshe and Lenard Goldesmyth were named as quarrelsome, common gossips verging on scandal-mongering. Their husbands were to keep them in order.

Polluting the water supply, bonfires near thatched houses, vandalism and gambling were all punishable offences and no one was exempt. We may well speculate what in 1410 caused Richard the chaplain of Lullokesburg to 'draw the blood of Laurence Scolemayster with his fist.'

By the sixteenth century Dunster had become a busy and prosperous woollen town. (See Chapter 5) It was a period of growth and consolidation marked by the building by George Luttrell in 1547 of the Yarn Market for the buying and selling of wool. The next century was to be far less settled.

Living beside a castle brought employment and prosperity. It also had its dangers. In 1138 Dunster Castle held by William de Mohun for the Empress Matilda, was besieged and eventually reduced by Henry de Tracy on behalf of King Stephen. In 1265 during the barons' wars Sir William de Berkeley with a band of Welshmen landed at Minehead prepared to lay waste the region. Adam Gurdon, the warden of the castle and supporter of the baronial cause, led a rebel force and put the invaders to rout. After the defeat of the barons at the Battle of Evesham, Gurdon was ousted from the castle held in wardship at the time by Queen Eleanor.

During the Civil War between King and Parliament (1620-1670) Dunster Castle was besieged again. From the start the Castle was a focal point of military activity in the West, both sides keen to hold a fortress so well-placed strategically. The Castle was held initially by Thomas Luttrell for Parliament but after some skirmishes in January 1643, Thomas was prevailed upon by Francis Wyndham to join the Royalist cause paying one thousand pounds perhaps as a fine, perhaps as an earnest of his intentions. He died in 1644 and his widow and son went to live at Marshwood in Carhampton.

In May 1645 the 15-year old Prince of Wales was sent from Bristol to Dunster to avoid the plague but his stay at the Castle was brief since plague was rampant in Dunster itself, 23 burials being recorded in that month. Many houses in West Street have communicating doors said to date from this time when people avoided going into the street 'where they might contract the disease.'

*West Street.*

In October 1645 Colonel Robert Blake, with 600 men, was ordered to Dunster to reduce the Castle which was being held for the King by its governor, Francis Wyndham. Blake made his headquarters in a 'strong house', the Ship Inn, now the Luttrell Arms Hotel. Wyndham was short of supplies and water but refused all Blake's demands for surrender and instead appealed to General Goring for reinforcements. Blake had no wish to storm the castle. He had drawn up his batteries behind the Ship Inn but even when he moved his trenches forward, his field guns were unable to make inroads in the massive medieval curtain walls and towers. Blake used miners from Mendip to undermine the walls in three places but hesitated to fire. When ordered by Fairfax to do so, only one mine did any damage and that in such an inaccessible spot that Blake felt no compulsion to attack.

Meanwhile Francis Wyndham was hard pressed, not only for supplies but for ways of defending the weakened walls. Early in January a Royalist troop made a surprise attack on Blake in his 'strong house' and out-numbering Blake's men, was able to destroy his 'trenches and batteries' and replenish Wyndham's supplies of powder and food. With their departure the siege continued.

Now the Royalists began to suffer defeat in the West Country and in mid-April, as rumours of Parliamentary successes began to reach the beleaguered men, it was decided by Blake and Fairfax that a final show of force might bring an end to the blockade. Blake and his men, with reinforcements totalling about 2000, drew up in full battle array on May Hill facing the castle and summoned Wyndham to surrender. On April 19th generous terms were accepted and after a siege of more than five months Sir Francis Wyndham and his men marched away from Dunster with drums beating, colours fluttering, musketeers at the ready, watched by soldiers from Cromwell's New Model Army and, surely with relief, by the townsfolk of Dunster.

The siege must have been a time of great anxiety with troops sta-tioned on the hills close by and skirmishes in the town itself. It is said that forty houses were burnt out during the siege. The Yarn Market was dam-aged and had to be re-built. (A cannon ball hole in one of the beams can still be seen.) We know little of the opinions of the local people but textile

workers and seamen tended towards puritanism and so supported Parliament. The New Model Army was well-disciplined and bought what provisions they needed. Some townsfolk may have done quite well by selling to the army and regretted the end of the siege but most, I expect, would be glad to be free of the danger in their midst and the constant fear of battle.

In 1685 the town was again involved in the thrill and horror of a national rebellion. In June that year the people's hero, the Protestant Duke of Monmouth, landed at Lyme Regis to challenge his Catholic uncle, James II, for the crown. As he marched north through Chard to Taunton where he was rapturously received, the Duke was joined by crowds of eager and innocent working men whose enthusiasm was to be no substitute for arms and fighting skill when they met the King's army under Lord Feversham on the Somerset Levels. Twelve Dunster men, mainly substantial tradesmen though their number included two doctors, joined Monmouth's march and were present at the disastrous defeat at Sedgemoor.

Of these men, Henry Luckwill, together with William Sully from Bridgwater, were hanged at Dunster. A third man, similarly sentenced, may have died of small pox in prison.

We can imagine the procession watched by silent and sympathetic townsfolk, making its way over the packhorse bridge to the gallows on Gallox Hill. Later the quartered bodies were 'disposed upon gates, bridges and crossways', a terrible reminder of the outcome of treachery.

During the 17th and early 18th centuries Dunster continued to flourish as a market town and centre of the woollen industry. The high spot of the year for many inhabitants would have been the annual fair. In her unpublished article, 'A Backward Look at the Market and Midsummer Fair in Dunster', Eleanor Crane writes:-

*'The eager visitor to the Fair could buy bread and cakes, breeches and bonnets, earthenware and silver, cutlery and hardware. She or he could replenish her store of rope, thongs and laces, saddlery and pewter; she could have pots and pans repaired by the brazier and the pewterer, buy shoes or boots, gloves and hats. The cooper was there selling*

*fine buttertubs and water barrels, the pedlars and piddlers with their baskets of ribbons, lace, stockings and buttons. Toys for the children, confectionery and gingerbread stalls were there in plenty, as were sellers of books and tobacco, fresh fruit and fish. Occasionally, there was a visit by a travelling quack doctor, and when the season was good, women with baskets full of nuts for sale. When the marketing was done there was the fun of the fair to be enjoyed and marvelled at. Puppet and other Shows amused the children, who readily gave their small money to dip into the Lucky Bag or spin round on the Whirligig. A man with a Wild Beast or a Bear was sure to appear, and the lotteries and "Will of the West" show amused child and adult alike. Bullocks and sheep, penned at the end of the Market Street, added their own sight, sound and smell to the cheerful melee of the Midsummer Fair.'*

By the end of the 1700's Dunster was changing. In West Somerset the woollen industry did not adapt to mechanisation, and competition from other parts of England soon brought a sharp decline in woollen production and trade. Writing in 1791, Collinson notes that there are one hundred and ninety houses in Dunster, some in a ruinous condition, but that at the beginning of the century there had been four hundred and that many woollen workers had moved away, presumably to the new industrial centres to find work.

*Dunster Toll House built soon after 1765.*

In 1765 Minehead Turnpike Trust was established by the local gentry, partly in the hope that new and improved roads would counteract this decline in industry and trade, prevalent in the whole area. A new road was built from Minehead through Alcombe to Dunster, on through Timberscombe, Beazley and Lype to Bampton. Other links were made with the Bridgwater and Taunton turnpikes but it was too late. Few people now visited Dunster market while by 1800 the Fair sold little in the way of essentials and was simply a Fun Fair. Streets and bridges fell into disrepair and the shambles became so dilapidated that in 1825 it was pulled down. The old Town Hall, Tub House, Corn Cross and stocks all disappeared though the Butter Cross was re-erected later on the Alcombe road where medieval Dean Lane meets Back Lane. The Yarn Market remained, a picturesque symbol of the past, its preservation hinting at Dunster's future.

*The Butter Cross.*

12

# CHAPTER 2

# Dunster Town The Nineteenth Century

By clearing away the remnants of Dunster's earlier greatness, the town was in a position to develop in new directions. In 1840 the Somerset Gazette Directory noted that as the former wool trade was wholly lost the population was 'dependent upon the retail business of the neighbourhood'. According to Greenwood, writing in 1822, of the one hundred and eighty three families in the town, eighty four were involved in agriculture, seventy eight in trade, manufacture and handicraft and twenty one in neither. Pigot's Directory of 1830 lists bakers,

*Dunster High Street about 1865 before the reconstruction of the castle. Part way down the street putts stand outside the butchers' shambles (1825). A little further on is the house used as a school.*

13

blacksmiths, butchers, carpenters, coopers, maltsters, millers, saddlers, tailors, tallow-chandlers, watch-makers, and wheelwrights to which can be added in 1840 dressmakers, a straw bonnet maker, tea dealer, nursery and seedsman and a chinaman. Versatility was the order of the day. William Vicary, postmaster, was also parish clerk and hairdresser; William Letty, auctioneer and clock-maker, was agent for the Atlas Fire Insurance and for the Somerset County Gazette while Worthington Vesey Prideaux who began life as a plumber, later took over the post office.

Dunster by 1840 had clearly turned its back on the old days of the cloth industry and the weekly market and was developing as a town of small businesses ready to serve the local neighbourhood.

A few families saw little prospect of success and left Dunster to seek their fortunes in Australia. Following the death of Thomas Markham, tailor and inn-keeper, Mary his widow, decided at the age of 60 to emigrate with her children; John, a saddler, whose wife Georgiana, came from Porlock; Henry , an agricultural labourer, and Margaret, a general servant. They were all able to read and write and John and his wife were Wesleyan Methodists. They sailed on September 14th 1851 on board the *Statesman*, bound for Geelong in Victoria. Two years later, another son, Thomas, a carpenter, with his wife Elizabeth and three children sailed on the *Stebonheath* to Newtown. In January of the same year, James Tudball, another Wesleyan, travelled with his wife, Hannah, through appalling flooding on the Somerset Levels, to Deptford, where they embarked on the *Monteagle*, bound for Melbourne, to work for Captain Buckley of Flemington. Their son, William Henry, was born in Cotham in 1855.

It is likely that these literate Wesleyan adventurers were among the first working people of Dunster to receive a regular education. In 1818 the vicar of Dunster, the Rev. G.H. Leigh, stated in the parochial return: "no school in this parish, poorer classes would be grateful for education." Six years later, William Moore, a respected Methodist preacher, left £800 to found a day school in Dunster. It was opened in premises in Mill Lane, close

14

to the chapel and manse, and when a new chapel was built in West Street in 1839, expanded into the old chapel buildings. It was the first Wesleyan Day School in West Somerset and one of the first to receive a government grant and regular inspection. It thrived and in 1853 was enlarged to accommodate 60 pupils.

*The front of the Wesleyan school premises in Mill Lane, now a private house.*

*West Street about 1850. On the left is the Methodist chapel and on the right a house demolished soon after.*

One or two small private, or 'dame', schools educated a handful of children in the town. Miss Elizabeth Harvey's Academy for Young Ladies existed for more than 20 years and took boarding pupils from some distance. However, it was the opening of the Wesleyan School which seems to have galvanised the Establishment into action.

By 1830, a Charity School had been set up, supported by the Luttrell family, with Mary Strong as schoolmistress. In 1851 John Jones and his wife Ann were master and mistress, and the school was probably occupying premises on the east side of the High Street. The school became known as Dunster Church of England National School and in April 1863, Thomas Moore, a certificated teacher and Principal of the school, started to keep a daily record of its progress. This log reflects his struggle to teach basic reading, writing, ciphering and religious instruction against the odds of consistent absence for potato-planting and picking, stone-clearing, bird-scaring, hay-making, harvesting, mushrooming, gleaning and picking worts - a reminder that half Dunster's families were still employed in agriculture and needed to supplement meagre incomes in every way possible.

Special occasions involved the master, too, and at a time when education was not compulsory, the school might be closed for Ploughing Matches, Minehead

*Harvesting in the 1920's.*

Hurdle Races, Cricket Week on the Lawns, Club Walks and Dunster Great Market. A visit by Womwell's Menagerie in July 1869 caused a sensation, not least because they refused to pay the turnpike toll and the elephant lifted the gate off its hinges to let them all through. Parish feasts to celebrate national events were held as early as 1856 when one was given to the people of Dunster to mark the end of the Crimean War.

Education was an issue close to the heart of the vicar, the Rev. T.F. Luttrell. He supported and taught in the school and ran a night school for boys and young men where they could learn to read. 'In the evening of his life', he 'signified his determination to build schools and a teacher's residence for the educational requirements of the Parish'. He was encouraged by Mr. George Luttrell

*Dunster School soon after opening in 1872.*

who gave the site and contributed to the costs. In 1872 the school was able to move to its spacious new premises near the church. Sadly the vicar did not live to see the opening when 130 children, preceded by a banner inscribed 'Dunster Church Schools' marched from their old school through the churchyard to the new schoolroom.

The school prospered, pupils walking from Carhampton and Withycombe to take advantage of its high standards. Gradually numbers at the Wesleyan School dwindled and in 1903 it was closed, the 20 remaining pupils being transferred to the National School.

*Digging for Victory in
the Second World War.*

The new school was only one of a number of
building projects begun at this time. The Castle was remodelled, the Parish Church thoroughly restored and the
Wesleyan Chapel re-built. The police station and
magistrates' court at the foot of Dunster Steep was built
in 1858 and the Village Hospital opened in 1867. The
West Somerset Railway was extended to Minehead in
1874 and a station built at Dunster Marsh. Several of the
larger houses were re-constructed with new frontages and
a few new houses were built. These schemes brought an
influx of workmen and new opportunities for
employment. Dunster's population rose from 983 in
1831 to 1156 in 1871 and directories record increased
numbers in building and related trades.

The last thirty years of the century were a time of
prosperity for the town with retailers, wholesalers and
craftsmen taking full advantage of the economic boom
initiated largely by Mr. Luttrell's investment in building
undertakings. With their rising standard of living many
looked to improve the amenities of the town and in this
they received every encouragement, financial and
otherwise, from Mr. Luttrell. Streets were surfaced,
water was piped to the town from Broadwood, gas and
electricity were laid on and by the end of the century the
streets were lit in winter by thirty oil lamps. In 1825 a
new butchers' shambles had been built in the High

Street near the Luttrell Arms Hotel and in 1874 a Reading Room was opened above it: newspapers were provided and a library of some 200 volumes made available to the parish. The opening of the railway provided new links with Minehead, Taunton and beyond while the daily coach between Minehead and Williton continued to call at the Luttrell Arms. The carrier called each week-day, adapting to the new transport by connecting with the statutory 'Parliamentary' train at Williton. The weekly journey to Exeter involved an overnight stop.

Not everybody was prosperous. From 1834 Dunster was part of the Williton Union and paupers were sent to the grim work house there. A number of Friendly Societies provided mutual support and a form of insurance against illness or injury, members paying a small weekly subscription and receiving benefit when unable to work. Dunster Tradesmen's Club owned a field between Frackford and Gallox Bridge which was leased to augment their income. A young men's Friendly Society was set up in 1871 and the Ancient Order of Foresters was well established by the 1870's when they held their annual walk and feast in the High Street.

*The Annual Feast of the Ancient Order of Foresters.*

In 1867 the Cottage Hospital was opened in a property leased rent-free from Mr. Luttrell on the sloping ground to the west of West Street, formerly known as Happy Valley. The hospital was financed by subscriptions, donations, collections and special events. The proceeds from the opening of Dunster Castle Gardens went to the hospital for many years. Both in-patients and out-patients were accepted, any out-patients attending regularly for treatment. Labourers, farm servants and the needy could be recommended for treatment by subscribers who for an annual donation of 10s could recommend one out-patient a year and for £1, two out-patients and one in-patient. The hospital catered for surrounding parishes as far apart as Porlock and Luxborough, and the clergy were able to recommend patients from these parishes. The hospital was run by a matron, and a surgeon and a dispenser were appointed annually, Samuel Ell holding the latter post for many years.

In 1896 it was decided to form a Fire Brigade. Donations were solicited from insurance companies for the purchasing of uniforms. The Imperial contributed £10 and the Norwich Union, three guineas. After receiving advice from the London Fire Brigade, uniforms were bought at two guineas a head including belt and axe. Only the officers seem to have had helmets together with silver buttons and red cuffs. Mr. Davis, the Captain, had red facings to his tunic. A board which once hung in the Tithe Barn listed the members of the brigade at the end of the century. The fire pump was kept in the stables at the castle.

Nearly half the population was still employed in agriculture; they worked both on the outlying farms such as Broadwood and Staunton Cross and on the farms still in the heart of the village, Priory Farm right beside the church and Home Farm, the farm of the castle. An

*Priory Farm.*
*c.1865-72.*

annual Christmas stock show and sale was established in 1835. The show was held together with the Roots Fair, on Waglands, the fields between Conygar and The Ball. The meat market was held in the High Street where the animals were penned near the building which had been put up in 1825 to house the butchers' stalls. From 1875 to 1886 monthly cattle auctions were held in the market place, special market trains being advertised with cheap fares available to bring customers to Dunster. After 1886 these monthly sales were held in Williton, but the Great Cattle Market continued in Dunster High Street on the first Friday of each December until 1925.

21

*Great Christmas Cattle Market. c.1907.*

Townsfolk were beginning to take a pride in their well-kept town and on more than one occasion wrote to the auctioneers, Messrs Hawkes and Risdon, to complain of the condition of the streets after the markets. By example and education, Victorian attitudes of thrift, self-sufficiency, unquestioning obedience and loyalty, were fostered. Dunster Penny Bank encouraged weekly savings while the Dunster and Williton Agricultural Society, besides helping to develop agricultural skills such

*Haymaking on Dunster Lawns. c.1912.*

as ploughing and bee-keeping, rewarded those who been in service longest with one master and those who had brought up most children without recourse to the parish.

In the early part of the century Dunster had six or seven inns, but the numbers dwindled and some like the

22

George and the Horse and Crook were turned into living accommodation though sometimes by a circuitous route which reflected the worthy aim of encouraging sobriety and even abstinence alongside profit as we shall see. In

*Keeping up a tradition of hospitality, these houses were once the George Inn.*

1879, Joseph Neades, the landlord of the Horse and Crook, was exhorted 'to extend custom but not encourage or permit drunkenness.' His successor, Henry Manning, died in 1901 and Mr. Luttrell considered selling the property to The People's Refreshment House Association. Their rules stated that 'intoxicants are not to be exposed with a view to attract customers but every means is to be taken on the other hand to expose food and non-alcoholic drinks so as to encourage their consumption'. Plans were drawn up with a small bar, large tea-room and no billiards room, but on investigation the Association realised the full cost of adapting the dilapidated house and rejected the offer. Hancock's Brewery offered for the property but Mr. Luttrell decided instead to lease it for an annual rent of £20 to a Miss James of Cardiff who had visited the area and decided she would like to live there.

*The old Horse and Crook Inn. The sign has been copied from the original.*

Miss James was one of a new class of resident leasing properties in Dunster round about 1900. Some had private incomes; others were members of the professions. Throughout the 1800's visitors to Dunster stayed at the Luttrell Arms Hotel remarking on its hospitality and visiting the church, castle and grounds. As the boom years ended and the population once again declined, the number of visitors increased and townsfolk began to turn their attention to providing meals and accommodation for them. A cyclist visiting Dunster in 1894 stopped at a cottage 'the mistress of which is willing to supply a simple meal, such as tea, new laid eggs, preserves etc. for not more than three or four persons at a time.'

Four years earlier J.Ll.W. Page wrote, 'Dunster is one of the few, the very few, thoroughly old-fashioned country towns, in this utilitarian nineteenth century, spared to us. Whether we look down upon it from the crest of Grabhurst, the grounds of the castle or from either end of its main street, the same appearance of almost medieval aspect is presented, the same restful air broods over it. Here are no hideous modern villas, glaring with stucco. In their stead quaint thatched or tiled houses, one or two rich with ancient woodwork

*William Clitsome 1817-1896 stands in the doorway of 5, The Ball with his four sons. His wife Elizabeth can be seen at the window. William was at one time gardener at Dunster Castle.*

under peaked gables, blink in the sunshine at the curious wayfarer.'

During the next sixty years in spite of two wars, the growth of transport and a steady flow of 'curious visitors' the pace of change was slow. The sale catalogue setting out details of the Dunster Estates in 1951 included a photograph of the High Street looking towards the Yarn Market. Trees are in full leaf, there are three parked cars, discreet signs advertising refreshments and post-cards and not a person in sight. The properties for sale included long-established businesses, a smithy and a saddlery, builders and a coal merchants, butcher, tailor, grocer and chemist. With a newsagent, post office and visiting bank the town was still virtually self-sufficient.

This has all changed. The essential Dunster still exists but the growth in leisure time and the current interest in things past have combined to turn the town into a tourist honeypot, and catering for the needs of the visitor makes economic sense. There are few businesses left which serve the needs of the town all the year round. Meanwhile residents and planners work together to ensure that the crowds of summer visitors neither obscure nor actually eradicate the very sights and atmosphere which they have come to enjoy.

CHAPTER 3

# Families at the Castle

Dunster Castle has been in the ownership of only two families, the de Mohuns and the Luttrells, from the time it was first built until very recently.

*Dunster Castle, a fairy-tale view.*

The first castle was built by William de Mohun soon after 1066. The tor was levelled, scarped for the top eighty feet (25m) and a simple but strong fortress and defences put up, probably constructed of timber. In building the first Norman castles the priority was speed so that they could be used in enforcing the Norman Conquest of England.

Gradually the walls and buildings were replaced in stone to form 'impregnable defences ... inaccessible on

25

DUNSTER.

the one side where it was washed by the tide and very
strongly fortified on the other by towers and walls, by a
rampart and outworks'. (*Gesta Stephani. Mid 12th
century.*) The sea has receded over the centuries.

Over the next 70 years the de Mohuns administered
their estates in Normandy and England profitably and
made generous gifts to churches and monasteries in both
countries. Gradually the de Mohuns acquired more
property in England and in 1204 when Normandy was
separated from England, Reynold de Mohun chose to pay

homage to King John since his chief estates were now English. Reynold de Mohun II (d.c.1213) built a new gate house at the castle (known today as the Gateway) and buildings for his own use in the lower ward of the castle. The great medieval walls can still be identified in the present castle. An extent of 1266 identified the buildings still in use on the tor: a hall with buttery, pantry, kitchen and bakehouse, a fair chapel, a knights' hall, three towers and a prison. The lower ward included three 'towers' or groups of buildings, and a granary. The cow-house, stable, dovecot and dairy lay below near the river.

During the next hundred years the de Mohuns proved powerful supporters of the Crown, fighting in wars in France, Wales, and Scotland and dutifully accepting the irksome burden of attending Parliament. Many of the de Mohuns died young and the Crown frequently benefited from their estates being held in wardship.

John de Mohun V (c.1320-75) inherited the estates when he was only 10 and when he came of age married Joan de Burghersh, daughter of his first guardian. John was a brilliant soldier. He fought at Crecy alongside Edward, Prince of Wales, in the division said to comprise 'all the flower of the chivalry of England.' The prince later presented him with a fine charger, Grisel Gris. John was one of the original twenty-five Knights of the Garter, but like many professional soldiers, he found it hard to settle at home. As a young man he was involved in various felonies in Somerset, imprisoned and only released after royal intervention. He moved in wealthy circles and lived extravagantly, well beyond his means. At home he seems to have been under the thumb of his wife, Joan, while his three daughters, who all made sparkling marriages, must have added to his mounting debts. As the likelihood of there being a male heir diminished, Joan seems to have decided to look to her own future. A series of complex and legally suspect transactions gave her a life interest in her husband's estates and the right to dispose of the Dunster properties. In 1374, even before her husband's death, she set in motion the sale of the reversion of the Dunster estates to Lady Elizabeth Luttrell for 5,000 marks, a transaction completed in 1376. When John died, Joan shut up the castle and moved to be nearer Court, the heart of the social scene which she much preferred to country life. She lived for a while in London and in Canterbury where she died and was buried in an ornate tomb in the Cathedral. She outlived the Lady Elizabeth.

The Luttrell family probably originated in France, for their name comes from 'loutre' meaning an otter. Geoffrey Luttrell (d.c. 1216) from Nottinghamshire was a supporter of King John, a trusted courier who frequently crossed to France on royal business. It was he who laid the foundation of the family fortunes by marrying the heiress Frethesant Paynell (Paganel). Their son, Andrew, inherited his grandfather's Paynell estates and successfully laid claim on the death of a third cousin, Maurice of Gaunt, to several manors in Lincolnshire and Somerset, including East Quantoxhead, always a favourite residence and still belonging to the Luttrell family.

Lady Elizabeth Luttrell who bought the reversion was a great lady in her own right, a grand-daughter of Edward I, a sister of the Archbishop of Canterbury and the widow of Sir John de Vere, son of the Earl of Oxford. She married, doubtless for love, into a junior branch of the Luttrell family and it was her son Hugh (c.1364-1428) who, on the death of Joan de Mohun, aware that the Dunster inheritance might be challenged, acted quickly to establish his claim. In spite of moves by the de Mohun daughters and their influential husbands, Hugh was able to establish the upper hand and by 1406 could feel sure of his inheritance. By then he had ousted the tenants from the castle and moved in  with his wife and household to celebrate Christmas 1405. Clean rushes were strewed on Christmas Eve; they feasted on venison, capons and pork and were entertained with music and dancing performed by townsfolk and children of Dunster and Minehead. It may well have been cold in the castle for the Luttrell ladies  ordered fur for their gowns and Hugh soon had glass installed in the windows.

Hugh Luttrell was a man of wealth and influence, the personal and trusted envoy of both Richard II and Henry IV. He fought in Wales against Owain Glendower and in France;  he eventually became Lieutenant of

Harfleur and Seneschal of Normandy, representing the English interest. Surviving accounts show that he and his family lived at the castle in style, surrounded by a retinue of servants dressed in colourful liveries with embroidered pockets. Meat, game and fish were bought for the lord's table, the latter often secured live and kept till needed in the fish ponds in the Hanger Park. There were purchases too, of imported luxuries; ginger and pepper, olive oil, almonds, dates, figs and raisins. Hugh restored the neglected fabric of the castle, securing doors, re-furnishing the kitchens and making all watertight with Mendip lead. In 1420 the new gatehouse was begun, which still stands. With its six smallish rooms, each with a fireplace, it must have been a comfortable addition to the older rambling buildings.

During the next century little was done to the castle. Hugh's heir died within two years of his father and the inheritance passed to his 4-year old son. Then in 1455 civil war broke out between the Yorkists and Lancastrians, rival claimants to the throne. James Luttrell, a strong Lancastrian supporter, went north to join the army of Henry VI. He was knighted on the battlefield of Wakefield but soon after was wounded at St. Albans and died five days later. As the Yorkists seized power, James Luttrell and fellow Lancastrians were charged with high treason and the Dunster estates declared forfeit and given to the King's favourite, William Herbert. James' widow, Elizabeth, was left homeless but soon re-married and was able to re-possess some of her inheritance. The remainder of the property was not recovered until the death of Richard III. Even then the Castle was not lived in very much; Hugh (d.1521) preferred East Quantoxhead, John (c.1519-1551) was away in the wars and Thomas (1525-71) lived at

*Sir Hugh Luttrell's Gatehouse built c.1420 photographed in c.1870 during the alterations to the castle.*

*The tomb of Lady Elizabeth Luttrell.*

Marshwood. Only Andrew (d.1538) lived in the castle for a while and almost certainly found it cold, inconvenient and old-fashioned.

George Luttrell (1560-1629) was to change that. He inherited at the age of eleven, became a Fellow Commoner at Caius College, Cambridge and was admitted as a member of Gray's Inn. He acquired a reputation for enjoying legal squabbles and being a 'Builder'. He married twice, both times to ladies disapproved of by his family. Joan, the daughter of his lawyer guardian, Hugh Stewkley, often at odds with the Luttrells, was described as 'a slutte' who had no good qualities while the termagant Sylvestra Capps,his second wife, was 'an obscure person from Wiveliscombe'. She obtained East Quantoxhead as her marriage portion and lived there with subsequent husbands who suffered, along with the servants from 'her wicked ways'. Her second husband in his will left 20s 'to Giles Baker, my servant, who hath lived under the tyranny of my wife, to the danger of his life, during the space of two years'.

George was responsible for building a new harbour in Minehead and the yarn market in Dunster, for re-designing what is now the Luttrell Arms Hotel and altering substantially the family homes at East Quantoxhead and Marshwood. He went on to convert the medieval jumble of buildings in the lower ward of the castle into a Jacobean mansion, quarrelling with his architect William Arnold over the cost and quality of the work. As we have seen, the new house within the medieval defences withstood attack during the Civil War, but for the Luttrell part in the Royalist cause an order went out to demolish it, and in 1650 a gang of one hundred men was sent in. They totally demolished the buildings on the tor, the towers and the curtain wall but a last minute order countermanding the first was just in time to save the dwelling house and Hugh Luttrell's Gatehouse.

During the Civil War, a political pamphleteer, William Prynne, was imprisoned in the castle for protesting against the execution of Charles I and denouncing the Parliamentary régime. For his earlier supposed attacks on the King and Queen and on the bishops he had lost both ears and had been branded on the cheeks, 'S.L.', seditious libeller. He was only allowed to speak with others in the presence of his gaoler but seems to have been given free run of the castle and spent his time usefully calendaring the 'confused chaos' of the Luttrell muniments. Prynne's work forms the basis of the catalogue of the comprehensive collection of Luttrell archives held in the Somerset Record Office.

Little was done to dispel the gloom of military occupation at the castle until 1680 when Francis Luttrell married the beautiful heiress, Mary Tregonwell of Milton Abbas in Dorset. They adopted a fashionable and sumptuous life style. Hundreds of pounds were spent on clothes for themselves and their children. Francis' uniforms were, according to his tailor, made of cloth 'much better than the other officers' and the male servants were arrayed in liveries with gorgeous trimmings of black and gold lace. The castle was altered to provide a fitting setting for this extravagance and the ornate plaster ceilings and elaborately carved staircase depicting stag and fox hunting scenes were installed at this time.

Francis led the local militia at the time of Monmouth's Rebellion and in 1688 raised a troop of foot in support of William of Orange. When the troop was incorporated into a regiment Francis Luttrell became its first colonel; the regiment was later to be known as The Green Howards. He died in 1690, only 31, and his widow took most of the furniture to her London house. Narcissus Luttrell wrote in his diary for 19th November, 1696, 'Yesterday morning a sudden fire hapned in Mrs. Luttrell's house in St. James's Street, being newly and richly furnished, which burnt it to the ground, the lady herself narrowly escaping and 'tis said she lost in plate, jewells, etc. to the value of £10,000'. A few weeks later Mrs. Luttrell married the Swede, Jacob Bancks, who is said to have rescued her from the flames. She died of smallpox in 1704.

Not surprisingly, Francis Luttrell left debts which were still being paid off in 1720 by his brother Alexander's widow, Dorothy, who on her husband's death, took up the management of the estates for her son. She had a reputation for kindliness and good sense and

was responsible for building an ornate chapel at the back of the castle and a new and easier approach road, besides repairing the harbour at Minehead.

Dorothy's grand-daughter, Margaret, inherited the Dunster estates in 1737 when she was 11. She was to make a wise choice of husband in her second cousin, Henry Fownes of Nethway in South Devon, for their marriage was happy and he was prepared to spend his own money to set the rocky fortunes of the Luttrell family

*Across the Park.*

32

back on an even keel. His portrait shows him as a solid and sensible country squire and his sensitive landscaping of the castle and grounds succeeded in enhancing his country way of life. The beautiful setting of the castle owes much to the vision of Henry Fownes Luttrell. He was interested in country pursuits, horses, hounds, and fighting cocks and created an ornamental deer park to replace that at Marshwood, Carhampton. He levelled the tor and laid a bowling green, employing an artist much esteemed by local families though described by Maxwell-Lyte as 'rather indifferent', Richard Phelps, to design the romantic bridges, arches and waterfalls near the mill, and Conygar Tower with its mock ruins now shrouded in trees. How grand it must have been to have a 'castle' at either end of the village!

*The Palladian Bridge.*

Palladian Bridge
below Dunster Castle

D.V. Jessup

Henry Fownes Luttrell took an interest in politics and nurtured the borough of Minehead so that it was largely back in the family pocket from 1768 until 1832 when the borough was disenfranchised by the Great Reform Act.

Henry's son John stood as Member of Parliament for Minehead and followed his father in managing the Dunster properties as a country estate but his sons John (1787-1857) and Henry (1790-1867) Fownes Luttrell were both unmarried and often away. The wife of a visitor to the castle in 1845 writes of the fine views but mediocre and old-fashioned furniture. Elizabeth Ernst

describes 'a sad picture of departed greatness,' the owner an inveterate bachelor, generally in London, while 'two old maiden aunts' lived in the castle in great seclusion. The stables and kennels were empty and the servants with little to do, 'twenty idle people'.

It is not surprising that very soon after George Fownes Luttrell inherited in 1867, he decided on a drastic reconstruction of the castle to make it a more comfortable place to live. He engaged the distinguished and experienced architect, Antony Salvin who, with sympathetic eye, remodelled the interior, by adding two new towers and a service wing to the old Jacobean house and successfully medievalised the exterior. He aimed to make the castle look and feel as if it had been constantly

*Reconstructing the castle 1867-1872.*

restored and improved - as it had been - rather than re-building in the style of one specific period.

The work was begun in 1867 and completed by the end of 1872. In January 1873 neighbouring gentry and clergy were invited to a ball at the castle along with tenants who paid an annual rent of £50 or more. For most of the guests this would have been the first opportunity to view the impressive restoration. Seven years later the Prince of Wales paid a private two day visit to the Castle, primarily for the hunting. He travelled by train to Dunster station where he was greeted by townsfolk who accompanied him to the castle between houses decorated with flowers and greenery.

The castle gardens had been well tended since the 1700's. In 1830 Savage remarked on the famous lemon tree, intrigued by the ingenious moveable frame which protected it in winter. A tree was in existence as early as 1759 when sailcloth was ordered to cover 'the frames of the lemon tree'. Fifty plum trees and forty quinces were planted in 1764-5 alongside numerous apple trees. In the eighties glass frames for cucumbers and melons were purchased and a green-house heated by an oil fired 'ingin' was repaired. The vegetable gardens were prolific growing every imaginable vegetable including collyflowers, hotspur peas, garlick, shot top radishes and cardoons. Cottage flowers such as sweet peas and nasturtiums were grown in the walled gardens in contrast to the shrubs and exotica planted close to the castle itself. In later years cockleshells were ordered by the ton to be used as fertiliser.

*Dunster Castle Gardens. On the left is Mr. Webber, Head Gardener at Dunster Castle 1887-1900.*

The castle grounds were open to the public from the 1870's in aid of the Village Hospital. Arrangements and fees varied over the years but in 1871 there seems to have been a two-tier system for visitors. Tourists changing horses or staying overnight at the Luttrell Arms Hotel might buy a ticket to view the gardens at any time save on Sunday and could buy a family ticket for 2s.6d if there were enough of them. However, respectable persons residing in the neighbourhood might only visit the gardens on Tuesday afternoons and had to pay full price for their cards of admission: 1s for two people.

George Luttrell and his successors took their responsibilities to their tenants seriously and many of the improvements made in Minehead and Dunster were initiated and in some part, at least, paid for by the family. Their concern and generosity is more marked when we realise that there was not money to spare; the property and estates were most carefully managed and even the tiniest source of income, such as rabbiting or wortleberry picking, could not be ignored.

When Alexander Luttrell died in 1944 he had not made over either castle or estate to his heirs. Crippling death duties were incurred and in 1949 Geoffrey Luttrell was forced to sell. The Ashdale Property Company bought the major part of the 8,600 acre Dunster estate in 1949 which was later sold to the Commissioners for Crown Lands. The Castle and grounds passed to Colonel Walter Luttrell on the death of his father (1957), who, when his mother died, gave the house, gardens and Old Park to the National Trust in 1976.

*Dunster Castle and Gardens are owned by the National Trust. Open from April to October. Please check opening times and charges by ringing 0643 821314. There is a large car park below the castle approached from the main road and a shop in the Castle Stable block.*

JOHN WYTHER

*The figures on the Wythers brass.*

AGNES WYTHER

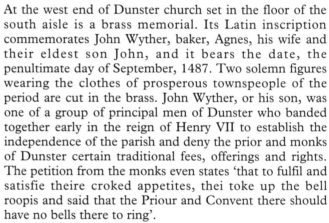

# CHAPTER 4

# Church and People

At the west end of Dunster church set in the floor of the south aisle is a brass memorial. Its Latin inscription commemorates John Wyther, baker, Agnes, his wife and their eldest son John, and it bears the date, the penultimate day of September, 1487. Two solemn figures wearing the clothes of prosperous townspeople of the period are cut in the brass. John Wyther, or his son, was one of a group of principal men of Dunster who banded together early in the reign of Henry VII to establish the independence of the parish and deny the prior and monks of Dunster certain traditional fees, offerings and rights. The petition from the monks even states 'that to fulfil and satisfie theire croked appetites, thei toke up the bell roopis and said that the Priour and Convent there should have no bells there to ring'.

It is unlikely that John Wyther and his fellows, Thomas Upcott, merchaunt; Thomas Kodogon, yeoman; Adam Wilkyns, clothemaker; William Crasse, bocher; Symond Pers, yoman; John Greyme, yoman; John Philippis, tanner; John Paynter, barbour; John Morgan, parker; Martyn Glover; saw the matter in this light. Dunster in the fifteenth century was as we have seen, a thriving market and woollen town. The burgesses and tradesmen were wealthy men, some managing their own businesses and travelling widely. Their Christian beliefs were deep-rooted but their independence and initiative led them to challenge the rights of the small group of monks, bound by rules and tradition, who dominated their church life and worship. They wanted more say in the governing of their church and to spend some part of their profits to the greater glory of God, by rebuilding the church as did their contemporaries in Gloucestershire and Suffolk.

38

The origins of this dispute and others which developed in the 1400's can be found in the earlier history of the church in Dunster.

Nothing is known of Christianity in Dunster before about 1100. Five hundred years earlier the people of the area were listening to the preaching of missionaries such as Carantoc, Decuman and Keyna who had crossed from Wales and found places to live near the coast. Their dynamic words and lives were responsible for the conversion of many; churches were dedicated in their honour and legends grew around their memory. The steps and stump of a cross in the churchyard at Dunster marks the place where preachers set up wooden crosses and spoke to the gathered crowds about Christ long before even the simplest church was built in the parish.

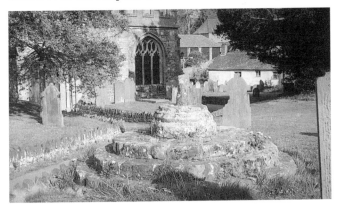

*The steps and stump - all that remain of Dunster's medieval preaching cross.*

Sometimes during the last decade of the eleventh century, the first William de Mohun gave the church of St. George at Dunster together with land at Alcombe, the tithes of several manors and two fisheries, one at Dunster and one at Carhampton, to the Benedictine abbey at Bath. Presumably there was by that time a small church in the town for these gifts were for the purpose of 'building and raising' the church, a task which was completed during the next century. The solid Norman work can still be seen in the west and north walls of the nave.

The Norman church was just over 80 feet (24m) long and nearly 25 feet (8m) wide, with a fairly flat wooden roof and a large round-headed arch at the east end leading to the chancel. There may have been a low tower. The monks from Bath Abbey responsible for building the church would have lived in basic accommodation while the important work of raising a church for the worship of God was being carried out. Once it was complete they would have been able to turn their attention to building something more permanent around the cloister set beside the northern wall of the church. The priory is first mentioned in 1177 and by the reign of John was well-established and able to provide accommodation, food and stabling for the Vicar of Dunster, Richard the Chaplain, who was not one of the monks but who was responsible for the needs and worship of the parish.

During the reign of Henry III the choir of the church was enlarged (now the much restored east end) and people gave generously to found and maintain chantries such as the chapel of St. Lawrence, mentioned first in 1254, at which prayers were said constantly for the souls of the departed.

From 1262 the Priory had a more distinct organisation. Its endowments were increased by the de Mohun family and the monks held and farmed a separate manor, a fair-sized area of land to the north of the Church and in Alcombe where they served a small chapel. In the south aisle can be seen the inscribed tombstone of Adam of Cheddar, prior c.1338-55, who was responsible for 'sumptuous buildings' which may have included the priory itself. At one point the dorter where the monks slept was close to the north wall and no doubt the usual nightstair led directly to the church so that the monks were able to reach the chancel for the night services without venturing outside. A walk way around the cloister garth would have been covered by a penthouse roof and here monks would have written at raised desks similar to the one with the sloping lid now used in the church as a chest. The present buildings known as the Old Priory were built in the later 15th century and housed the prior's lodgings together with kitchens and storerooms.

In 1357 the difficulties of sharing a church building began to emerge. An agreement was made in that year between the prior, Richard of Childeston, the monks and the parishioners who, on Sundays, were to unite in one procession and then all attend the conventual high mass at the altar of St. George in the chancel where the parishioners would make their offerings four times a year. On festivals the vicar might say a simple mass beginning part-way through the high mass at the Holy Rood altar, almost certainly positioned on the screen between the western arches of the nave as it was later.

At mass the parishioners would stand in the nave and it is easy to imagine that they would feel dissatisfied and cut off from worship led at the far end of the church and separated from them by screens. Other clauses of the agreement referred to the provision of candles, expensive at the time, and the division of responsibilities regarding the upkeep of the building.

In 1420, William Pynsoun, 'citizen of Dunster' bequeathed 6s. 8d to the work of the new Rood Loft, 40s. to the building of the new bell-tower and 20s. for a new bell. This work was evidently begun soon after, for in 1443 a contract was drawn up between the churchwardens and John Marys, a builder of Stoke Courcy, for finishing the bell-tower by adding two further stages to the work already begun. The tower above the 'grass-tabyl' was to be 100 feet (30m) high; it was to have three French buttresses and a 'vice' or staircase in the fourth corner. Four windows in the belfry were each to have two lights separated by a 'moynell' and divided by a 'trawnsom' designed by Richard Pope, freemason. The main walls were to be 4 feet (1.25m) thick up to the 'bell-bed' and 3 feet 6 inches (1m) above. There was to be a 'batylment', three 'gargylles' and four 'pynacles'. The parish would provide materials and equipment and Marys was to receive 13s. 4d. for workemanchyppe and 20s. extra for carving the pinnacles. Once the tower was complete a rood loft was put up between the western arches of the tower. The doorway leading to it from the new tower staircase can still be seen. It supported the altar of the Holy Cross used regularly in parish worship. Another screen with doors leading to the chancel crossed between the eastern arches. A new roof, almost flat, with carved bosses and massive ribs, was placed over the Norman nave and work was done in the north and south transepts by both monks and parishioners.

Soon after this, trouble blew up again between priory and parish and in 1498 matters were taken to arbitration in Glastonbury and an agreement reached, which effectively divided the church into two parts. The monks were to occupy the east end and the vicar and parish the west where they were to 'build and maintain' a new and separate choir though this was not expected to supersede the High Altar at the east end. An immediate result was the construction of the wonderful carved rood

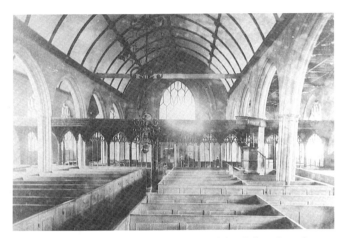

screen which crosses the whole breadth of the church two bays west of the tower. This section became the new parochial chancel. But before this could be completed the nave had to be reconstructed, the south aisle enlarged and the nave roof replaced by the present waggon roof. The earlier roof seems to have been adapted to cover the south aisle. The north aisle was rebuilt soon after 1504 when Thomas Upcot left 10 tons of iron 'to the new aisle there to be built or repaired on the north side'. The west window was installed in about 1530 together with the octagonal font, its delicate carving depicting the five wounds of Christ and the instruments of the Passion.

The dual use of the church established in 1498 did not last long for in 1539 Dunster Priory was dissolved and John Leland visiting Dunster soon after 1540 wrote 'The hole church of the late Priory servith now for the paroche church. Aforetymes the monks had the est part closed up to their use.' The priory buildings and lands passed into the hands of the crown and were at first leased by John Luttrell (uncle of young John Luttrell who had recently inherited the castle) who lived in what was to be known as Priory Farm beside the church. In 1543 the property was sold but bought by John Luttrell's sister-in-law through an agent and remained in Luttrell hands. The rectory, the tithe receipts and the responsibility for appointing a vicar, was also leased by John Luttrell at first but was soon conveyed through various hands to Hugh

Stewkley who in 1566 was accused of not making proper provision for a curate although he was receiving the tithe income. The lack of provision for a priest continued as a problem in the parish, there being a minimal endowment to support a clergyman, until 1872 when a new vicarage was built and the cure properly endowed.

Eventually these responsibilities passed to the Luttrells and by 1643 the chancel was no longer used for parish worship but had become a burial place for the family who had their private chapel at the castle. It is conceivable that the parishioners preferred the spacious nave to the old priory church which was rapidly becoming dilapidated. As late as 1703 timber and tiles were still being taken from the 'cloister court', some being sold for building purposes, some used for church repairs but all regarded as the property of the parish. It seems that there was never a clear distinction between what belonged to the parish and what belonged to the castle.

However neglected the church seems to have been at the end of the seventeenth century there was always

*Dunster Church before restoration c.1872. In the background is the new vicarage. Notice the perpendicular window at the east end soon to be replaced. The walled gardens of the Castle spread out between church and tithe barn.*

Charlie Thrush rings the daily bell in the 1920's. Now known as the Angelus Bell it has rung morning and night for 300 years to mark the beginning and end of the working day.

William Long, 1819-1884, Parish Clerk.

plenty of money spent by the parish on the bells which were rung to mark a variety of occasions: the death of William's Queen, Mary; the coronation of George I; the peace of Utrecht; all to the accompaniment of gallons of beer. Ropes and clappers often had to be replaced but in 1684 one of the bells was re-cast in a furnace somewhere between Loxhole and Conygar and maybe near the pottery kiln behind the Luttrell Arms Hotel where there was a building named on the Tithe Map of 1843 as the Bell House. Later bells were carted to Watchet or Minehead and then shipped to Bristol for re-casting.

In 1717 a gallery was put up at the west end of the nave to accommodate musicians and singers, and in 1728 £40 was paid to Richard Phelps, the Porlock artist and Luttrell protégé, for restoring the altarpiece.

THE ARTICLES OF RINGING

I   You that in Ringing take delight
    Be pleased to draw Near
    These Articles you must observe
    If you mean to ring here.

II  And first if any Overturn
    A Bell as that he may
    He forthwith for that only Fault
    In Beer shall sixpence pay.

III If any one shall Curse or Swear
    When he come within the door
    he then shall Forfeit for that Fault
    As mentioned before.

IV  If anyone shall wear his Hat
    When he is ringing here
    He straightway then shall sixpence pay
    In Cyder or in Beer

V   If anyone these Articles
    Refuseth to Obey
    Let him have nine Stripes of ye Rope
    And to depart Away

*William Gale, John Withers*
*Churchwardens 177(1)*

There followed a period of neglect which seems to reflect the downturn in the town's fortunes. Both Collinson in 1791 and Savage in 1830 spoke of the dilapidated state of the church and particularly the chancel. In 1838 the architect S. C. Buckler surveyed the building and in cryptic language condemned the church as ruinous, damp, draughty and dangerous. The nave was filled with a hotch-potch of box pews, 'the most promiscuous, unseemly and uncomfortable assemblage of pews that can be met with'. It is little wonder that the worship of the time had little dignity. Prebendary Hancock, vicar of Dunster in 1905, reported stories of unseemly behaviour by the lads in the gallery who were corrected by a rap of the sexton's stave, and of the clerk, William Long, seated in the stall below the pulpit, who would announce the metrical psalm in sonorous tones, then mount the gallery to take up his bass viol alongside the two fiddles, flute and violoncello which accompanied the choir in complex contrapuntal hymns and psalms. Once the singing was over he would return to his stall before the service could proceed.

*The Methodist Chapel in West Street c.1900. The New Inn is now the Stag's Head.*

This gloomy state of affairs together with the economic problems of the people, provided fertile ground

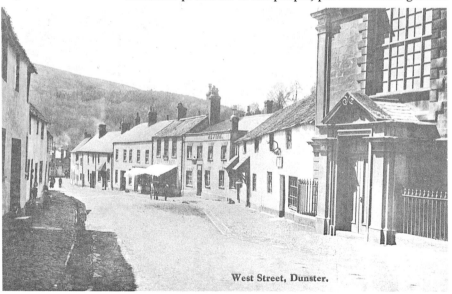

West Street, Dunster.

for the Methodist evangelists. Rowland Hill preached in Dunster in 1771 and by 1809 a Methodist meeting was established. In 1811 premises in Mill Lane were purchased and a chapel was built. The meeting flourished and in 1832 a plot of land on the corner of West Street and St. George's Street was bought. The shops and unfinished cottages on the site were incorporated into a new chapel and for some years the cause thrived encouraged by the conversion of Mrs. Langdon, the personal maid of the two Miss Luttrells at the castle. With the revival of fortunes in the town and the generous interest of Mr. George Luttrell in the church and school, Methodism lost ground. The chapel had to be rebuilt in 1878 but soon after, the Wesleyan day school closed and only a small, but loyal membership remained during the present century. The chapel closed in 1968.

Following Buckler's highly critical report a minimal amount of repair work was carried out in the church including the installation of a Bryson organ in the West Gallery replacing the instruments and choir whose music was now considered vulgar and rubbishy by church reformers. Then, in 1875, a complete restoration was begun under the sensitive guidance of the architect G. E. Street ably assisted by G. H. Samson who saw the work through. These days the restoration might have been done differently, but as Francis Eeles wrote, 'Very great care was taken of every detail and Mr. Street's new fittings are marked by dignity and restraint.' A large perpendicular window at the east end was removed and replaced by three thirteenth century lancet windows constructed from remains found in the vicinity of the church by Mr. Samson. The west doorway was enlarged and new choir stalls enclosed by screens, were put up in the Priory church. The gallery and box pews were removed and a new high altar was set up under the central tower a little to the east. The screen once crossing between the eastern arches of the tower was moved to the curiously shaped thirteenth century arch in the south transept, which had been widened in the fifteenth or sixteenth century. The Bryson organ was moved to the north aisle where it was pumped by a complicated hydraulic system. When this failed, a hand pump was installed.

The medieval altar stone in the Priory church was found upside-down in an aisle and restored to its rightful position. Whether it had been overturned for safe-keeping during the Puritan occupation of Dunster when it is said that the church was used as accommodation by the soldiers, or cast on one side when altars were ordered to be replaced by communion tables in 1550, we shall probably never know.

Since the restoration, Dunster Church has been well cared for by the priests and people of Dunster, encouraged particularly by Dr. Francis Eeles who wrote an excellent church guide and ran the Council for the Care and Preservation of Churches from premises in Dunster High Street.

*'In my end is my beginning.'*

# A Visit to St. George's Church, Dunster

It is best to begin a visit to the church from the lych-gate at the top of the church path. From here the churchyard, fringed by old buildings and studded with stones remembering townsfolk long gone, stretches down to the red, sandstone church. On the left are the remains of the priory buildings, now private houses. Half way down to the right of the path are stone steps and a stump, all that remains of a medieval cross. Beyond is a spreading yew tree, symbol of everlasting life and thought to drive away storms raised by witches. The ornate north door replaced a plain arched doorway when the church was thoroughly restored in 1875 by W. H. Samson under the guidance of the architect G. E. Street. In the corner of the churchyard near the gateway into Church Street is the old Priest's House, re-built in 1875 and often inhabited in Victorian days by the parish clerk.

Enter the Church through the porch built about 1500.

On going into the church for the first time the thing that impresses most is the near-tangible atmosphere of calm. The church, though much altered, is the oldest building in the parish and has been central to the lives of Dunster people for at least 900 years. They have come at the turning-points of their lives, in the joy of marriage or christening and the grief of bereavement; in peace and war, bringing personal hopes and fears, nagging anxieties and fervent thanks – all the fragments that make up the patchwork of human existence.

There are many interesting and beautiful things to see in the church, yet it is not a museum but a living building sustained by daily worship. Visitors are always welcome to join this worship and to add their prayers to those offered here over the centuries. Everyone, whatever their belief or non-belief, will find an antidote to the speed and stress of modern living in the peace and quiet of the building.

Once inside the main door it will be hard to resist the temptation to walk to the centre of the nave and take a first look upward to the wide waggon roof (c. 1500) and eastward towards the altar of the parish church and beyond.

After these first impressions, return to the main doors and turn to the west. At the back of the south aisle is the octagonal font (c. 1530) with delicate carving that

*Delicate carving on the octagonal font.*

shows the instruments used in the crucifixion of Jesus and the wounds inflicted on his body. In the floor close by is a brass with two incised figures commemorating John and Agnes Wyther (1487). Above is a fine roof, once part of an earlier roof to the nave. Move again to the centre of the nave. Turn your back on the screen and look to the west. The oldest part of the church, the Norman walls, can be seen in the north and west walls of the nave. The restored door we have already looked at from the outside. On the north wall is a Royal Coat of Arms of 1660, commemorating the restoration of the monarch, Charles II, who when Prince of Wales, spent a night at Dunster Castle during the Civil War.

Turn to face east and you will see the exceptional fan-vaulted rood screen, the longest in England. It was built about 1500 and placed here, two bays into the nave, to form a chancel for the parishioners, separate from that of the monks of the Benedictine priory. The rood screen was so named because it usually supported a wooden rood (or crucifix) with figures of S. Mary the Virgin and S. John on either side. The projection in the centre at the back was to support an altar which was reached by a staircase set in the wall of the south aisle. The van-vaulting is deceptive. If you stand directly under the screen you will realise its full width and strength.

Make your way to the eastern end of the church through the south door in the screen. Earlier screens once stood under the tower and the doorway at the head of the stairs leading to one of them can be seen in the N.W. pillar of the tower. In the south transept is the grave-stone of Adam of Cheddar, Prior of Dunster c. 1345-55, which was discovered in a fire-place in the post-office. Between the transept and the aisle of the Priory Church, probably once the chantry chapel of S. Lawrence, is an arch of c. 1240 which was widened at the bottom in the fifteenth or sixteenth century. The screen crossing it dates from c. 1240 and was once part of the screen under the eastern arch of the tower.

*Detail of the fan vaulting.*

In the aisle are three interesting wooden chests. One has a slanting lid and is though to have been used originally as a desk, perhaps in the priory. Another is a dug-out chest of perhaps the twelfth century. The third, probably thirteenth century, is secured with iron bands. The last two each have five hasps and when they were used to house the parish valuables, five padlocks kept all safe. The five keys were held by the vicar, the two churchwardens and the two overseers of the poor, and all had to be present to unlock the chest, a simple ruse to deter dishonesty. Against the south wall is an impressive monument with three recumbent figures: Thomas Luttrell and Margaret Hadley of Withycombe, his wife,

*Widened arch with former rood screen.*

*Parish papers and valuables were once stored in this thief-proof chest.*

and their daughter-in-law Joan Stewkley. George Luttrell who put up the monument on the death of his wife is shown kneeling. It is dated 1613. Set in the floor at the east end is an alabaster slab with an incised effigy and inscription to Lady Elizabeth Luttrell dated 1493. Both monuments were moved here during the church restoration. On the north wall is a memorial tablet to Henry Maxwell-Lyte, keeper of the Public Records and Historian of Dunster.

The choir of the priory church which is used for daily worship was thoroughly restored in 1875. Above the altar, with its medieval altar stone inscribed with five consecration crosses, are three thirteenth century lancet windows restored with fragments replacing the perpendicular east window which can be glimpsed in early photographs.

On the south wall is the effigy of a lady, probably Christian Segrave, wife of the fourth John de Mohun (c.1325). On the north side of the sanctuary are the mutilated effigies of Sir Hugh Luttrell (d.1428) and his wife Catherine Beaumont (d.1435). These lie on a much restored altar tomb with canopy (c.1500) which was probably designed for use as an Easter Sepulchre.

Return to the nave of the parish church noting the brass plate of the alms box dated 1634 with the initials of the churchwardens, Matthew Haite and John Giles. In the north aisle the organ and trumpeting organ pipes dominate. Set in the floor is a brass plate economically commemorating first Edward Poyntes (1583) and later in the eighteenth century the three daughters of Giles Poyntz.

A doorway in the N.W. pillar of the tower leads to the ringing chamber where visitors are welcome on Thursday evenings during practice hours.

A door in the north transept (with a tendency to bang!) leads into the scented air of a garden set in the cloister of the old priory.

The great tower, about one hundred feet high, looms overhead. It was built in 1443 and from it at one,

*Treble's going; she's gone!*

five and nine o'clock, day and night a carillon plays one of a number of tunes chosen in 1876 by Mr. George Luttrell. A gate in the wall leads back to the road near the dovecote and tithe barn.

Mr. Gladstone visited the church in January 1877. It is noted that he expressed his admiration for the restoration work and 'was particularly struck with the combination which our church presents of grandeur with simplicity and . . . that everything connected with it should be of the best . . . Such testimony as this from one so qualified to give an opinion is very gratifying'.

# CHAPTER 5

# The Working Community

## The Woollen Industry

When John Leland visited Dunster on his travels in 1538, he noted 'the toun of Dunestorre makith cloth'. More than three hundred years earlier the woollen industry was well-established in the town as the occupations listed in an extent of 1266 show. Adam the dyer, Walter the webber, William the fuller, Alice the webber and Christina the webber were all specialists in aspects of making cloth, an industry which involves a number of complex processes that in the early Middle Ages were all 'hand crafts'.

First the wool was 'carded' or combed and then spun on a distaff and spindle. The spinning wheel came into use later. The yarn was then woven on a loom worked by hand and foot and finally the resulting loose 'web' was fulled, again by hand or foot. Fulling involved beating the cloth in water, sometimes with the aid of fullers' earth, tallow and burned bracken which cleaned away the natural oils and shrank and felted the material. Cloth was then stretched out to dry in measured lengths held by tenterhooks on wooden racks or tenterbeds. Finally the cloth was finished; the nap was raised with teasles and sheared. Dyeing could be done at the yarn stage or after the cloth was woven; vegetable dyes were used including madder (red), sphagnum moss, weld (yellow) and woad (blue).

At first families made their own cloth but as specialisation developed so did the cloth industry. It was first based in towns alongside other specialist crafts but in the thirteenth century the mechanisation of the fulling process, replacing feet with a pair of wooden hammers driven by a water wheel, caused the industry to shift to rural areas where fast-running streams would power the wheel. It was probably for this reason that in the early 1200's the woollen industry expanded in Dunster; the first fulling mill is noted in 1259.

By 1430 there were at least four fulling or tucking mills in Dunster all situated at the western end of the town where a leat already provided the water to drive the lord's corn mills. This leat seems to have been utilised by the new mills, for in 1376 William Taillour built a new fulling mill over the lord's water course. Thomas Touker's mill was under Grabbist at Frackford and the Abbot of Cleeve had a mill in West Street perhaps on the site where there was later a grist mill. Others were at unidentified sites, le Colverhay and Parlebienshey but the name 'Toukerstrete' implies that they were all situated fairly closely together. A little later another mill was built on the river east of the castle. Trade was good during the fifteenth century and to get the work done fullers were ready to contravene the ordinance forbidding the mills to work on Sundays. During this period there were numerous tenting beds or racks on the slopes of the castle tor and Grabbist Hill.

Little is known of the type of cloth made in Dunster at this time. Lady Margaret Luttrell bought 'fustyan' and 'tatterys' for a double gown for herself in 'the market place at Dunsterre.' She also bought linen cloth, and russet cloth from William Stone who seems to have been a general merchant and may have brought the cloth from elsewhere. The accounts show that cloth was purchased from many sources. There is also an order in 1431 for a quantity of white cloth for the livery of my lady which clearly was made locally since the weaving, fulling, dyeing and shearing are all itemised personally. John Dyer was also paid for dyeing a bed-cover, hangings and cushions for 'my lady's hall and the chamber and the chapel at Karampton'.

Short-cuts which lowered the quality of cloth produced in the town reflected on everyone's business and were punishable offences. William Morgan was charged with mixing 'flokkes' with the pure wool in his cloth while John Lenchelond used thistles instead of teasles to raise the nap. Dyeing was a messy and smelly business needing a constant supply of clean water. With so many manufacturers using the same watercourse an order had to be made in 1492 forbidding the pollution of the lord's river with waste 'wodewater' before eight-o-clock each evening. By dawn the dirty blue water would have flowed out to sea.

The organisation of the industry varied, but by the seventeenth century was centred around wealthy clothiers who had money to invest. There were independent spinners who bought their own wool and sold their own yarn direct to weavers at the Yarn Market built in

*Pack animals crossing Gallox Bridge.*

Dunster in 1601. Others were employed by clothiers who bought and distributed the raw wool and collected the finished yarn. In the 1700's the yarn of Carhampton and Porlock spinners was particularly prized. The yarn was woven by weavers who in some places banded together in guilds to enforce standards and for mutual protection. After the fulling and dyeing, clothiers would employ men to dress and finish the cloth. Sometimes the clothiers leased fulling mills and racks and so were responsible for nearly all the processes from raw wool to finished cloth. The will of Stephen Fox, clothier, who died in 1688 is one of several Dunster wills which mention racks, shears, pressing planks and other tools of the wool trade. These entrepreneurs went on to market the cloth and their wills also mention shop counters, beam scales and weights and parchment skins for accounting.

Various sorts of cloth were made in Dunster at different times but in 1607 an Act of Parliament laid down regulations which standardised the kersey-type cloth known as Dunsters. It stated 'That every broad cloth commonly called Tauntons, Bridgewaters and Dunsters made in the western part of Somersetshire, or elsewhere of like making, shall contain, being thoroughly wet, between twelve and thirteen yards, and in breadth seven quarters of a yard at the least, and being well scoured, thicked, milled and fully dried, shall weigh thirty pounds the cloth at least'. Broadcloth made on a broadloom needed two weavers to cope with the greater width.

Not long after George Luttrell built the Yarn Market, the woollen industry in Dunster seems to have suffered a set-back and although there were periods of apparent recovery the overall trend for the future was

*The Yarn Market built by George Luttrell in 1547.*

downward. In 1621 a number of rackroomes leased from George Luttrell are all said to be decayed yet by mid-century a piece of waste-land was being beaten out of rocks at the lower end of West Street below 'Rack Cloase' and being used for racks. The numbers of racks and value of their rents fluctuated, but in spite of a few good years in the early 1700's the number gradually diminished, racks were taken up and destroyed and well-established lessees like John Perry and Nathaniel Ingram found themselves in arrears and their racks eventually taken up. After 1764 racks no longer feature in the Luttrell rentals.

Nathaniel Ingram probably leased the grist mills in West Street that had been put up by Colle on the site of the Abbot of Cleeve's fulling mill and may have used them for fulling as well as grinding corn or malt. When Henry Fownes Luttrell obtained the mill from Ingram in 1765 he converted it for fulling but an initial annual return of £15 was soon to fall to £8 in 1779.

Tracing the history of each fulling mill is complex and far from complete. John Burnell leased the house and fulling mill at Frackford near the bridge in 1682 and William Leigh took over the same property in 1713. Both had the right to set up racks on Grabbist Hill. Members of the Hossom and the Coffyn families leased other fulling mills during this period.

The decline of the industry was slow but sure in the eighteenth century. Collinson writing in 1791 spoke of one hundred and ninety houses where there had been four hundred and of a near-defunct industry that had succumbed to competition from the north. As people moved away the racks and mills were given up. Sometimes the property and land was turned to other uses; in 1733 a mansion was built on the site of a fulling mill in West Street; but in some cases they were simply abandoned. Beside the road to Timberscombe not far beyond Frackford Bridge on the right hand side is a copse in which can be seen all that remains of one of Dunster's fulling mills and the leat bringing the water to power it.

### Dunster Mill

Corn mills at Dunster are first mentioned in Domesday Book when there were two worth 10s. to the lord, William de Mohun. The mill played an important part in the economy of the medieval manor, all tenants having to take their corn to the lord's mill to be ground. The mill would be leased to a miller who would take a percentage of the corn ground for himself.

In 1329 the two mills were known as Overmylle and Nethermylle and were leased to a burgess, Walter Rughe, for an annual rent of £16. In 1405 the rent was set at £10 on the condition that the lessee was responsible for all repairs. Newmylle was built in 1427 by William Person who already leased the older mills. By 1620 Newmylle and Nethermylle were united under one roof

*Newmylle and Nethermylle were united under one roof by 1620.*

on the present mill site and known as Lower Mill. Overmylle or Higher Mill was presumably further up-stream but it had disappeared by 1779.

In March of that year the mill lease was advertised and included, 'All those complete set of Grist Mills known by the name of Dunster Mills with a very good newly erected dwelling house thereto adjoining and also proper stabling, Hogsty and other useful conveniences.' A most condescending application was made by Daniel Heald of Spittlegate who referred to Dunster as 'a little country place with nothing of a flour mill.' His offer of £5 a year annual rent was given short shrift by George Gale, the Luttrell agent, who soon negotiated a lease with a Mr. Mills of Bristol, who was to be allowed to make the improvements and alterations he wished, always remembering that Dunster Mill was in full view of the park and that Mr. Luttrell expected alterations to be done 'uniform' and 'agreeable to his good liking'. The mill, together with the nearby bridge and adjoining arch, formed a picturesque feature in Henry Fownes Luttrell's landscaping of the castle grounds.

*An appropriate drawing on George Gale's account book 1778-1779 giving details of repairs to Dunster Mill.*

Comprehensive repairs to the mill began in 1779 and were completed three years later but Mr. Mills did not stay to reap the benefits. The lease passed to John Bryant in 1782 and in 1801 to John Harvey who in 1802 insured the mills for £2,500. A valuation made in 1838 reflected a slump in trade. 'It is clear that trade has suffered because of the erection of new flour mills in the neighbourhood which have deprived Mr. Harvey of many of his best corn dealers, causing reduction in trade.' The mill remained in the Harvey family until 1875 when the business was taken over by Thomas Evered.

*The lord's leat carried water to drive the town's mills.*

The profitable running of a water mill depends on a regular supply of water and this had always been a matter for dispute in Dunster. In the second half of the fifteenth century there are several ordinances forbidding people to throw anything in the stream which might block the flow during the working week. The pressure of demand on water by the numerous fulling-mills and dye-houses limited the flow to the corn mills, positioned almost last on the leat, and rights· to water were sometimes questioned. In 1721 there was a long-drawn out dispute over the supply to Madam Luttrell's Mault Mill and Tyrrol's Tucking Mill. Evidently the tucking mill wouldn't work when the malt mill wheel was running.

In 1883 a long-standing wrangle between the Dunster miller and the family at Knowle House, who, in summer, diverted water for irrigation, came to a head. The final straw came one day when yet again there was no water and the stones ground to a halt. William Evered, who managed Dunster Mills for his father, strode up to Knowle in fury to open the sluices. His greatest crime as set out in a letter from Colonel Wynch to Mr. Luttrell, was not that he interfered with the irrigation but that he walked in front of the drawing-room windows in full view of the Colonel's guests.

Gradually the mill was worked less and less. In 1909 H.C. Maxwell-Lyte, Dunster's erudite historian, remarked, 'The wheels often stands idle nowadays, the lessee James Phillips having a more important mill at Minehead.' Long before this, the mill, in its picturesque

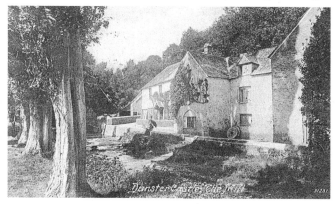

*Dunster Mill c.1900.*

setting, had become the haunt of artists and photographers and even Maxwell-Lyte waxed near-lyrical, in his description of the mill 'Nestling amid lofty trees immediately under the precipitous slope of the Tor, and close to a clear stream fringed with dock-leaves and meadow-sweet ... ' In the late 1930's visitors paid half-a-crown for 'permission to sketch in Mill Walk'.

The necessity for national self-sufficiency during the Second World War led to the repair and re-opening of the mill. A bakery on the premises supplied bread, baked with local flour, to castle and town. When peace came, the mill was confined to grinding for animal feed. It closed in 1962 and in 1975 was given to the National Trust by Colonel Walter Luttrell.

*The mill before restoration.*

The mill stood, silent and neglected, until it was leased in 1979 to Laura and Arthur Capps who, aided by grants from the Manpower Services Commission, the Historic Buildings Council for England and the National Trust, supervised a restoration to working order. The mill was opened to the public in February 1980. (For opening details see page 64.)

### The Pottery Kiln

In the garden of the Luttrell Arms Hotel, situated on the battery earthworks thrown up during the Civil War, is the shell of a pottery kiln now used as a garden shed. It is all that remains of a pottery run in conjunction with the Luttrell Estate brickworks which were established on the

Warren round about 1750. The pottery works were said to be 'in the old park' in 1759 and were doing good local business between 1758 and 1770.

*The pottery kiln.*

In 1775 an advertisement for the pottery was placed on the Bristol papers.

'A Pottery Work where is exceeding good clay and fuel plenty for making the coarse ware. Situated near several towns and above 20 miles distance from any other work of the kind, is to be lett.

Or a good hand well-skilled in making and burning such goods and can be well recommended will meet with great encouragement to carry on this work by applying to George Gale at Dunster near Minehead in Somerset.'

The brick and pantyle yard was also advertised.

Although the pottery was offered on lease - an earlier advertisement specified seven or fourteen years - it seems to have been worked by itinerant potters helped by local workmen. In 1758, Mr. Symons, the potter lodged in Dunster for just over three weeks and in 1761, the expenses were paid of James Norris, 'a potter coming from Crock Street to take the work.' The potters were paid for the work they did; lodgings were provided when necessary and there was a generous liquor supplement for all which was augmented during the very thirsty work of firing the kiln or 'burning'.

The potter was a highly skilled person, responsible for all aspects of the work: digging the clay, making the goods, supervising the building, packing and firing of kilns, delivering goods to individuals and local retailers and packing goods ready for shipping to wholesalers.

John and Ruth Mogg of Bristol prepared and fired seven kilns between 1759 and 1760 and Ruth managed a shop where the finished goods were sold. Following John's death, he was buried in Dunster on November

63

21st 1760, his wife was left to settle up the business and accounts with Henry Fownes Luttrell. Mogg may have been responsible for the brick yard as well as the pottery for both were advertised to let in 1760.

A wide range of domestic earthenware was produced including platters, pots and porringers, pitchers and pitkins, not to mention bowls for washing and pans for commodes.

The pottery may have been given up quite quickly but the brick yard was run as a profitable venture until about 1919, making bricks, tiles and pipes at competitive prices, for use in the many local building enterprises.

*Places to Visit*

*Exmoor National Park.*
*Dunster Information Centre.*
*Open every day, April -*
*October 10 a.m. - 5 p.m.*
*(0643 821835)*

*Dunster Doll Museum,*
*Memorial Hall, High Street,*
*Dunster.*
*A large and interesting*
*collection of dolls.*
*Details of summer opening*
*from the Information Centre.*

*Dunster Water Mill,*
*Mill Lane, Dunster.*
*A working water mill,*
*museum and shop.*
*Open April to October 11*
*a.m. to 5 p.m. daily (except*
*Saturdays). July, August*
*every day.*

CHAPTER 6

# Dunster Tales

Dunster is a great place for stories. Some of these stem from misconceptions, written down by early travellers and chroniclers, then given the force of truth by repetition in later guide-books. For instance, Bat's Castle, the Iron Age fort, used to be called Caesar's Camp and is still sometimes referred to as the Roman Camp not because of any firm evidence of Roman occupation but because 'Roman' seems at one time to have been synonymous with 'very old'.

A current story tells of the supposed secret tunnel running underground from Conygar Tower to Dunster Castle; an astonishing feat of engineering. Another tale describes a cupboard hidden behind plaster in the wall of a cottage near the foot of the tor. When it was opened up silver utensils were discovered which, so the story goes, 'belonged to the Luttrell family, and of course, were handed back at once.'

The opening up of communications between the West Street houses during the plague of 1645 is a long-established and dearly held tradition. The Archaeological Journal of 1858 includes this note from a correspondent in Bridgwater. 'The occupants of the several tenements in a long street ... established communications throughout its extent by opening doors internally from house to house, so as to avoid all necessity of going into the open street where the air was considered dangerous to life.' This is delightfully referred to as an early 'Sanitary Regulation'. The position of several of these doorways can still be identified in the party walls of a number of West Street houses. The openings would certainly have been utilised during the nineteenth century when flexible letting of houses seems to have been practised. A growing family needing more space was able to annexe rooms from an adjacent house occupied by only one or two elderly people while larger houses sometimes accommodated more than one family.

There are few giants in Somerset folklore but Dunster can claim one, the benevolent giant of Grabbist. He came up from Cornwall to Exmoor, so the story goes, to escape his unruly cousins. At first the townsfolk were afraid but once they realised the giant meant no harm they became quite fond of him and finding that their cattle and sheep were thriving they even began to worry about what he was eating. It turned out that the giant was fond of fish and he would wade out into the Bristol Channel and scoop up huge shoals of fish for his supper. Local fishing boats learnt to follow in his wake and made wonderful catches.

One day, when the 'Dorcas Jane' captained by Elijah Crowcombe had made such a catch and was filled with fish right up to the gunwales, a sudden storm blew up. The ship was tossed hither and thither and it was feared she would sink but the Giant stepped out, picked her up and popped here down in Watchet harbour all in a moment.

Back in Dunster, the Giant's reputation grew. He'd return from sea, sit down on the hill dangling his feet in the River Avill on either side of the castle and wash the Severn mud off his legs. Then he'd climb to his chair on Grabbist. Folk would look out of their windows and wave to him 'and 'e'd wave back and there was all the week's washing - dried!'

### Wassailing

Apple wassailing, the custom of visiting orchards to scare away evil spirits and ensure good crops, is still practised each year in the orchard of the Butcher's Arms in the neighbouring village of Carhampton on January 17th, Old Twelfth Night. After the singing of the wassail song, guns are fired into the trees, hot spiced cider is passed around and toast, soaked in the mull, is placed in the branches 'for the robins'. In Dunster the custom was carried on in a similar way until the 1950's. The story goes that one year the wassailers in an inebriated state, wassailed a pear tree by mistake and after this humiliation the custom was allowed to lapse.

66

### The Hobby Horse

On May Day evening the Minehead hobby horse visits Dunster. In the earliest printed reference to the custom, Savage in the Hundred of Carhampton, writes, '... they never fail to pay a visit to Dunster Castle, where, after having been hospitably regaled with strong beer and victuals, they always receive a present of money'.

*The Hobby Horse in West Street, Dunster c.1905.*

The origins of the horse probably lie in the ancient May Day fertility celebrations though it has been suggested that the horse commemorates a wreck or a phantom ship or was used originally to scare away Viking raiders. It consists of a wide wooden frame which is

*Wassailing in Dunster. The guns are fired and toast is placed in the tree.*

carried on the shoulders of a man whose identity is concealed by sacking brightly decorated with coloured circles and tassels of cloth. This is surmounted by a central beribboned head with grotesque face and conical hat. Gullivers, similarly dressed, and musicians accompany the horse which cavorts to the ceaseless drum-beat and compelling accordion melody known simply as The Hobby Horse Tune. Like the Pied Piper the horse attracts adults and children alike, who follow, their fascination tinged with fear.

The customary visit to Dunster is still practised although the Luttrells no longer live at the castle.

The Minehead Sailors Horse has sired a number of progeny and for a while Dunster had a horse of its own but it has not survived.

### The Ashen Faggot

The custom of burning the ashen faggot used to be observed at Christmas in many West Country homes. Legend says the custom originated after King Alfred's victory over the Danes at Ethandun when the conquering army feasted in the warmth of burning faggots of ash cut from the surrounding woodland. Another version is that the ash was cut and burnt after King Arthur's legendary victory at Cath-Brigion in Somerset.

The actual faggot was a bundle of ash sticks, bound with whips of ash or thorn, cut to fit the great open fireplace. As the faggot burnt the bonds would snap, wishes were made and toasts drunk.

*On Christmas Eve in the Luttrell Arms Hotel the ashen faggot is still burnt with ceremony and merriment.*

68

# Dunster Marsh

The part of Dunster lying to the seaward side of the main road is known as The Marsh. In medieval times a road known as St. Thomas's Street and later as Rattle Row, led from the top of the High Street, past St. Thomas's Chapel and rows of cottages to Dunster Marsh; that part of the town devoted to the sea, ship-building and fishing.

It is uncertain just where the sea-port was sited. If the sea once reached the tor, small ships may have tied up there. What is certain is that the river and estuary silted up and the centre of activities shifted to the old river mouth. The river has now been diverted and channelled to control flooding.

On either side of the river lay marshland, some used for wild-fowling, some as common grazing land. In the middle of this, near the river on a firm piece of ground, was a house of some importance now known as Lower Marsh. As early as 1266 Agnes of Marsh held a furlong of land for which she paid a rent of sixteen capons at Christmas and Easter.

*Lower Marsh.*

In the 1400's the wealthy Ryvers family lived at Marsh. John, as woodward to the Luttrells, held a house and twenty acres of land. He paid among other dues, the sixteen capons. His brother Robert was bailiff and steward and was in a position to advance large sums of money to Dame Margaret Luttrell.

The house passed to John Loty whose family held the property for three centuries. The first John Loty was constable at the castle and the family retained these links of service. At the end of the century John Loty III was the largest holder of burgages in Dunster and maybe his wealth made him unpopular. One violent day in 1487 after Hugh Luttrell's pound at Nether Marsh was broken into and twenty ewes stolen, a group of men prepared an ambush for John Loty with the intention of murdering him. It was unsuccessful.

The earliest parts of Lower Marsh and the Chapel over the porch were probably built at this time.

John's successor, Robert Loty, left a widow Joan who married, as her third husband, John Luttrell who lived for a while at the Priory after its closure. They were granted a divorce and Joan married yet again but John Luttrell does not seem to have let her go easily. He is said to have persecuted her, stealing sheep, killing doves, raiding the house for goods and flooding the lower part of the house by breaking down nearby dykes. The family was boycotted and, though some of the acts may be fictitious, John Luttrell's description of Joan as the supposed 'wyeff' of Peter Fauntleroy throws light on the episode.

The Chapel was in use at this time, for Joan had a domestic chaplain though John prevented him from saying mass by carrying off the chalice.

In 1510 the whole estate passed to the Poyntz family of Devon, Roman Catholics, who owned property at Leigh Barton and Leighland and contributed to the maintenance of a Benedictine priest there. They continued using the chapel at Marsh.

By 1760 their lands in Dunster and Carhampton had been let for some years and it was decided to sell them and the house to Henry Fownes Luttrell for the paltry sum of £2,400. Today the house at Lower Marsh with many interesting internal features is run as a guest house.

In 1874 the West Somerset Railway was extended to Minehead from Watchet. The line, broad gauge, crossed the Marsh and a station was built by William

Harrison for £912. Much of the ballast for the line was provided from the Castle Estate. The line was converted to narrow gauge over the last weekend in October 1882 and in 1897 the Minehead Railway was amalgamated with the Great Western Railway. Regular trains brought customers to market and took shop and office workers and school children to Minehead and Taunton. Holiday makers travelled by train from all over the country directly to Dunster. In 1971 the line was closed but opened again as a private concern in 1976 by the West

*Dunster Beach, hawn and chalets.*

71

Somerset Railway Association who run steam hauled trains in addition to diesel during the summer months.

Many of these holiday-makers who travelled by train stayed in the chalets on Dunster Beach, 'mini homes from home' which bring nostalgic memories of idyllic holidays and which are still in use today.

*Dunster Station.*

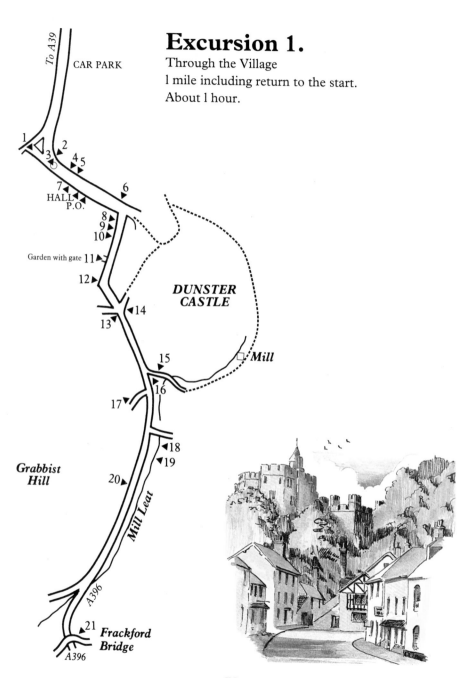

# Excursion 1.

Through the Village
1 mile including return to the start.
About 1 hour.

To A39

CAR PARK

1
2
3
4 5
7
HALL
P.O.
6
8
9
10
Garden with gate 11
12
14
13
DUNSTER
CASTLE
15
Mill
16
17
18
19
Grabbist
Hill
20
Mill Leat
A396
21 Frackford
Bridge
A396

73

This excursion follows the main streets through the village so is best tackled in the early morning or evening when there is less traffic. It is designed to help identify some of the more important places mentioned in the text.

The excursion begins on the Ball (1) just behind the Yarn Market where the old Corn Cross once stood. Climb the footpath behind the Yarn Market so that you have a clear view of the High Street with the Castle beyond, dominating the town. On the right of the Castle the highest trees on the tor mark the site of the motte where the first keep was built by William de Mohun soon after 1066. Today's silhouette was designed by Antony Salvin when the castle was finally remodelled in 1872. The street where the cars now park was the town market-place - it was once Chepyng Street and later la Market Strete. A row of wooden buildings or shambles housed market stalls and were pulled down in 1825. The butter cross (see p. 12) stood at the far end of the street.

On your left stands the Luttrell Arms Hotel (2) traditionally the guest house of the Abbot of Cleeve Abbey at Washford. Once three houses, by 1651 it had

*The Luttrell Arms Hotel.*

become the Ship Inn, and in 1786 Richard Phelps, the Luttrells 'artist-in-residence', painted a new sign which was resented by other landlords (preferential treatment?) and vandalised. In 1777 it was rebuilt as the Luttrell Arms Hotel and became a coaching inn with a consistent tradition of hospitality.

Walk down to the Yarn Market. (3) Dunster was a thriving woollen town from about 1250 to 1750. (See

74

*Carving on the court yard wall of the abbot's kitchen in the Luttrell Arms Hotel.*

Chapter 5)   This market house was built by George Luttrell for the sale of yarn and cloth in 1547 and restored in 1647 after being damaged in the siege of Dunster Castle. It is said that a hole in one of the beams was made by a stray cannon ball. Merchants would have spread their cloth on the wide wooden counters.   The building was prefabricated - look for the Roman numerals on the beams.   The bell in the turret used to announce the opening of the day's market.

Many of the houses in the High Street are on the same sites as the medieval burgesses' houses but have been altered, raised and in some cases given new

frontages. On the left a shop (4) carrying the name of Dyer was a saddler's from 1840 until recently; (5) is John Luttrell's butchers' shambles built in 1825 to replace those pulled down. The Bantam Shop (6) was the National School from c.1850 to 1872. On the right hand side look out for the sign of the Horse and Crook (7) an inn until 1901. The crook saddle had hooks from which bundles could be hung.

At the foot of the High Street turn right into Church Street. Beyond the Cage (8), (le Cornershoppe in the fifteenth century and once timbered,) the Nunnery (9) holds pride of place: a three storey, jettied building with two tiny medieval windows high up in the east wall. The house has a chequered history. In 1346 the site was granted to the Abbot and Convent of Cleeve by Hugh Pero of Oaktrow and the house was probably built soon after. At the Dissolution of the Monasteries it was sold and in 1620 bought as 'the High House' by Robert Quirke of Minehead. First rented as dwellings, in 1781 the building was used as a malthouse. It has never been used by nuns and the name may be just a flight of eighteenth century fancy based on a misunderstanding of the terms of the original grant.

Next door is Dollins' House (10) once occupied by

*Patterns on the Nunnery.*

*Samuel Ell outside his shop. Next door is the Nunnery.*

77

Samuel Ell, apothecary, dispenser at the Cottage Hospital, and maker of marmalade extraordinaire, found on breakfast tables in the Houses of Parliament. In 1866 Mr. Ell was preparing his celebrated algae sauce from laver which combined with 'several other wholesome stomachics rendered it a most delicious and agreeable relish far superior to most other sauces.' Some of these houses have no back entrances and horses once reached their stables at the rear through the main doors and wide stone-flagged halls.

If you are not in a hurry this may be the moment to visit the Village Gardens (11) entered through gates on the right of the street. This land was granted to the monks by the de Mohuns, and soon after the priory was closed in 1539 the land was bought by Lady Margaret Luttrell, eventually becoming the kitchen garden for the

*In Dunster Village Gardens.*

Castle. The gardens are now carefully tended by volunteers on behalf of the Dunster Village Trust.

Returning to Church Street you next pass the much-restored Priest's House at the entrance to the churchyard. The arch in the churchyard wall (12) may have been used to house a shop stall in the days when the road was lower, but it was more probably a water outlet for use by the townspeople. Water was channelled from St. Leonard's well into the town in medieval times. (See p. 94)

Turn now into West Street. At the junction with St. George's Street is the Methodist Chapel (13) rebuilt

in 1878. Opposite is Spear's Cross (14) named after the cross that once stood at this junction. You are welcome to view the model houses in the garden. In medieval times houses stretched up the street towards the castle, while West Street, the lower end especially, was busy with weaving, fulling and dyeing cloth. Many of the houses are linked by communicating doors said to date from the outbreak of plague in 1645 when people were afraid to go outside. (See p. 65)

Continue down West Street to the junction with Mill Lane. (You may like to follow the leat down to the mill which is working and open to the public (see pages 58-62). In the daytime in summer it is possible to return to the High Street through the castle gardens.)

On the left is the original Methodist chapel and schoolroom (15) while opposite are the almshouses (16) used to house the poor from c.1740 to 1839 when the

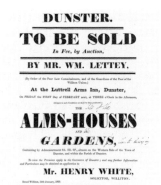

DUNSTER.

**TO BE SOLD**

In Fee, by Auction,

BY MR. WM. LETTEY,

(By Order of the Poor Law Commissioners, and of the Guardians of the Poor of the Williton Union;)

At the Luttrell Arms Inn, Dunster,

On FRIDAY the FIRST Day of FEBRUARY next, at THREE o'Clock in the Afternoon,

THE

**ALMS-HOUSES**

AND *the*

**GARDENS,**

Containing by Admeasurement 84. 2R. 5P., situate on the Western Side of the Town of Dunster, and within the Parish of Dunster.

To view the Premises apply to the Governor of Dunster ; and any further Information and Particulars may be obtained on application to

Mr. **HENRY WHITE,**

SOLICITOR, WILLITON.

Dated Williton, 14th January, 1839.

WHITBREAD, PRINTER, WATCHET.

houses were sold to William Symons. Dunster became part of the Williton Union and after 1834 paupers were sent to the workhouse there.

*Stray animals were penned in the pound and only released on payment of a fine.*

Continue down West Street and note the entrance to Grabbist House, once the Cottage Hospital.(17) Opposite the Foresters Arms, formerly the Bridge End Inn and thoroughly re-styled, were once more small cottages crammed beside a narrower road at the foot of the slope. Three of these were known as Apseys in 1708 and were used to house the parish poor. In medieval times the land here was a vineyard. On the left (18) was the grist mill which belonged in 1760 to Nathaniel Ingram (see p. 58) Beyond is the gated yard which was the village pound (19) where stray animals would be impounded and only released to the owner on payment of a fee. Opposite is the old toll house. (20)

The leat runs beside the road and can be tracked to where it was tapped from the stream. Beside Frackford Bridge (21) is a milestone and behind can be seen the remains of the old bridge. Near here stood Frackford House and Fulling Mill with racks for dyeing cloth nearby on the slopes of Grabbist Hill.

*Frackford Bridge.*

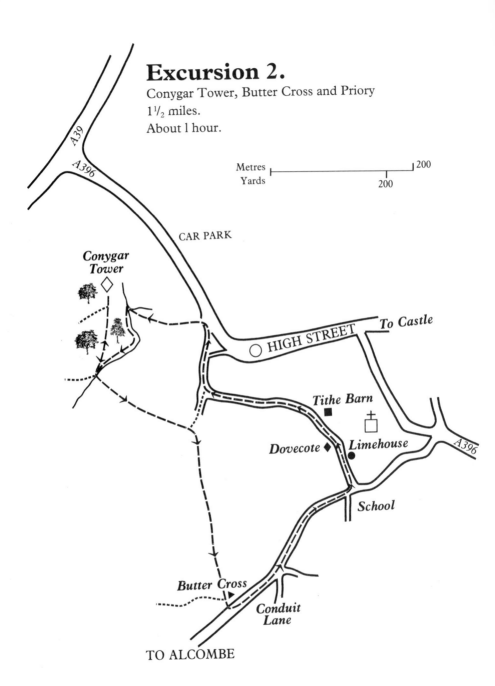

# Excursion 2.

Conygar Tower, Butter Cross and Priory
1¹/₂ miles.
About 1 hour.

Metres
Yards

200

200

CAR PARK

*Conygar*
*Tower*

*To Castle*

HIGH STREET

*Tithe Barn*

*Dovecote* ◆

*Limehouse* ●

A396

*School*

*Butter Cross* ▶

*Conduit*
*Lane*

TO ALCOMBE

This excursion begins at the Dunster Steep car park. There is a short climb to the tower and stout shoes or trainers are advisable. If you prefer not to visit the Tower, join the track which leads west from the Ball at the top of the High Street.

*Conygar Tower built as a folly in 1775.*

When you leave the car park turn left towards the village. Very soon turn right and follow the path which runs up beside the house at the end of St. Thomas's Street. Over the stile, cross the field to a second stile and enter the wood. Turn left and follow the path until another, leading from the field on the left, crosses. Turn right and climb to the Tower.

Conygar Tower was built as a folly by Henry Fownes Luttrell of Dunster Castle in 1775. It cost him £76.11.0½d. Scrumpy to keep the workmen going cost £4.2.6d while an entertainment for them when it was all finished was another £2.5s. An artificial ruined gatehouse lies to the west of the tower but beware

*The artificial ruins on Conygar Hill.*

straying off the main paths - there are steep-sided quarries nearby. Conygar was the medieval 'coney-garth' or rabbit warren.

Retrace your steps to the edge of the wood where the paths cross, climb over the stile and continue downhill across the field to a track. Turn right and go through the gate at the end into a field. Follow the footpath up the slope. On the horizon to the left you can just make out the earthworks of the Iron Age Camp, Bat's Castle. Below it the roof-tops of the town with the church tower appear curiously dwarfed.

At the top of the field you will emerge beside the shaft of a medieval cross raised on steps. Tradition identifies it as the Butter Cross that once stood at the foot of Castle Hill in the High Street, where farmers' wives from the neighbouring farms would have gathered to sell their dairy produce.

A red way-marked path leads down towards the main road, the medieval Dean Lane. To the right the road leads to Alcombe, once part of Dunster parish. Turn left down the hill. Note the grille in the wall protecting a deep well. To the right, a footpath, Conduit Lane, leads to St. Leonard's Well. (see p. 94) Continue downhill past Victorian houses until you reach thatched cottages and the school. Turn left into Priory Green, passing new houses built on gardens formerly belonging to the Castle. The high arch marks the entrance to the

*The lime-house.*

85

*The Dovecote.*

Benedictine priory precinct (see Chapter 4) and on the right is the lime house where lime, burnt in the kilns at Alcombe, was stored for use on the land and in building.

Follow the road as it curves round. The houses on the right were the prior's lodgings. On the left is the dovecote, recently restored. It was a part of the Priory property and provided fresh meat throughout the year: either squabs (young birds) or adult pigeons. There are about five hundred nesting boxes set in the wall reached by a ladder attached to a central pivot. The birds left the dovecote through the louvres in the 'glover' on the roof and must have proved a pest to those with crops growing nearby.

The dovecote, with the rest of the Priory lands, was purchased for the Luttrell family soon after the closure in 1539 and an entry in the Castle garden accounts in 1788 notes the purchase of a 'wyer lattice' in the pigeon house.

Entrances to the cloister and village gardens are on the right and ahead is the sixteenth century tithe barn where the tithe, or tenth of people's produce payable to

*The Tithe Barn.*

the church, was stored.

Pass through the second arch and follow the road back to the Ball at the top of the High Street. On the right the wall marks the limit of the medieval burgesses' holdings or burgages (see p. 4), now houses and gardens.

# Excursion 3.

Gallox Hill, Bat's Castle, Dunster Deer Park

About 3 miles.

1³/₄ - 2 hours

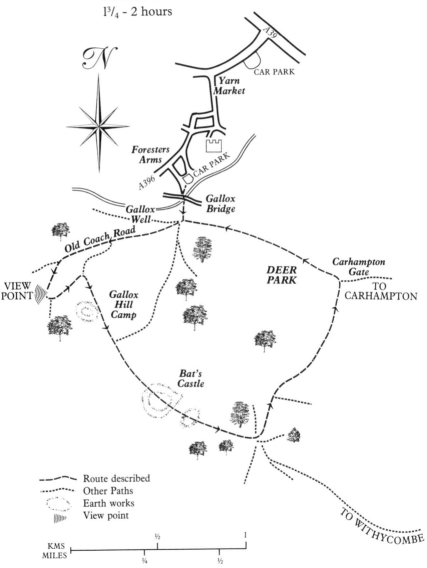

*A39*

CAR PARK

*Yarn Market*

*Foresters Arms*

*A396*

CAR PARK

*Gallox Bridge*

*Gallox Well*

*Old Coach Road*

VIEW POINT

*Gallox Hill Camp*

*DEER PARK*

*Carhampton Gate*

TO CARHAMPTON

*Bat's Castle*

TO WITHYCOMBE

— — — Route described
.......... Other Paths
Earth works
View point

KMS
MILES

½          1

¼          ½

The first mile is a steady upward walk with one short steep section. Some of the paths are stony and there is a damp area to negotiate so stout shoes or trainers are advisable.

*Cottages in Park Street.*

The excursion begins at the car park at the bottom of Park Street. Turn left between thatched cottages and cross the stream by Gallox Bridge, built for pack animals to carry their goods, high and dry, to and from the town.

Continue until you reach a gate and the junction of several paths. This is Gallox Cross where the main roads leading to the town converged, a probable site for the medieval gallows after which many nearby places are named.

Do not go through the gate but take the second track to the right through the woods until it reaches a clearing with a fine viewpoint on the right. Soon after it bears to the left. The track is known as the Old Coach Road and was part of a projected carriage-way devised by Mr. George Luttrell in the nineteenth century to run from the castle to the Luxborough road and beyond. It proved costly so the road was terminated at the viewpoint which became a popular place for picnics.

Just beyond the clearing a track joins from the left at a sharp angle. Take this track. As you approach a gate turn right and follow the footpath through the gap in the hedge, up through the wood and out onto Gallox Hill.

As you near the crest of the hill the first of two Iron Age encampments is on your right. This is a smallish but beautifully sited hill slope enclosure built originally as a safe retreat for isolated hill-top settlers and their flocks. It is well worth exploring.

Follow the path, past the point where a track joins from the left, up onto Bat's Castle, a larger Iron Age enclosure built later  (c.250 B.C.) to resist more serious attacks.  Although the earthworks have been raided for stone the ramparts are still impressive.  Imagine them topped with strong wooden walls while stout gates stopped the entrances. The entrance on the eastern side protected by parallel ramparts may have been added during the Civil War.

There are magnificent views from the ramparts across the Bristol Channel to Wales. Local weather lore says that if you can see Wales clearly it will soon rain; if you can't see it clearly it is raining.  To the south-east are the Quantock Hills, to the south-west nearby Croydon Hill and in the distance to the west Dunkery Beacon. Minehead shelters below North Hill which is partly hidden by the range ending in Grabbist Hill above Dunster.

When you have explored Bat's Castle, continue S.E. on the track which passes between defensive earth works that may be linked with the Civil War.  Go straight on through a conifer wood to a gate with a stony track beyond.  Turn left and continue downhill until the track bears sharp right.  Enter the Deer Park through the gates on your left.

The Deer Park, created by Henry Fownes Luttrell in 1755, was part of a landscaping scheme designed to enhance the castle and its surroundings. It also ensured a supply of game and venison for the castle table.  There were two earlier parks:  the medieval Hanger Park, close to the town wall where there was a large fishpond for storing fish, and a deer park  at Marshwood in Carhampton.  Once the land for the new park had been acquired, a fence and ditch was built all around  (a note of how many wooden palings were needed still exists) and deer were driven  from Carhampton along a specially constructed route through fences and gardens and lined solidly by virtually every man, woman and child from Dunster, Carhampton and Withycombe.

The footpath follows the course of the ancient road from Dunster to Carhampton used from at least the time

*Looking across the Deer Park to the Castle.*

of the Romans (Roman coins were found beside it in the last century) until the new park was formed.

Continue on the footpath, through a gate until you reach Gallox Cross once more. As you approach the Cross it is easy to envisage the River Avill as tidal. The estuary would have extended inland as far as Gallox Bridge, making it possible for small boats to tie up at the foot of the tor - an hypothesis yet to be proved but which ties in with a medieval description of the sea lapping the castle hill.

*The end of the walk in c.1872.*

Cross over the stile at the end of the track. Before returning to the car park you may like to visit Gallox Well, a short distance along the lower path signed to the main road. This has provided a supply of pure water to the town since the fifteenth century. A scheme was drawn up in the early eighteenth century to pipe the water from this and two other springs along lead pipes to cisterns in the town. One such cistern lies underground near the shop by the churchyard wall.

# Excursion 4.

Grabbist Hill, St. Leonard's Well

2¹/₂ miles.

About 1¹/₄ hours.

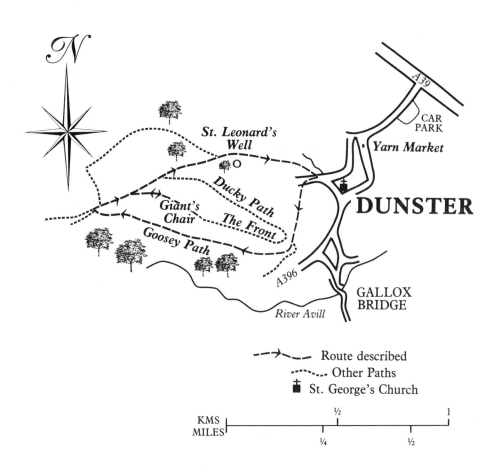

This excursion has one short steep section. Paths are stony in places and the track below St. Leonard's Well is very wet so stout shoes or trainers are advisable.

This excursion begins at the church lychgate. Take the path between the school and the thatched cottages.

Bear left between the allotments and the cemetery and follow the path until it reaches the wood. Behind are unusual views of the town's roof-tops.

Turn left on the yellow way-marked path and soon bear right uphill on Goosey Path once known as Goose Wheekes or Checkes Path. On the slopes below the path pieces of fulled woollen cloth were once stretched to dry on racks or tenterbeds. Further along, grapes were once grown in terraced vineyards.

Follow the path as it climbs the hill through the oak wood. Many of these trees were once coppiced to provide bark for tanning leather in the tanneries at Alcombe and Carhampton.

When you reach the junction of four paths turn right to follow the red way-marked path. On the left are extensive views of North Hill and the Bristol Channel. When you reach a gate on the left take the right fork through shrubland to the open hill-top. On the right is the Giant's Chair, a slip just below the edge of the hill. (See a story of the Giant on p. 66.)

From above the Chair are magnificent views of the Avill valley and Croydon Hill beyond. Avill Farm below was a separate manor once owned by the Aclands of Killerton, Devon and Holnicote near Selworthy.

It is not advisable to continue along this track to the Front unless you are very sure-footed; it is extremely steep. Instead, retrace your steps to the junction with the red way-marked path and turn right. At the entrance to the wood, ignore the right fork and follow the wall downhill. Where the path emerges from the wood turn right.

On the right under a medieval canopy is St. Leonard's Well. Water was once carried in wooden or later, lead, pipes to the priory and through the churchyard to the arched conduit in Church Street. Follow the path from the Well to the road which is known as Conduit Lane.

Take the main road down the hill. Opposite, behind a grille in the wall is a well fed by St. Leonard's Spring. The road passes between houses built in Victorian times, before leading back to the lychgate.